McGRAW-HILL LANGUAGE ARTS

Language Support

Grade 3   Lessons/Practice/Blackline Masters

McGraw-Hill
School Division
New York   Farmington

Table of Contents

Grade 3

Introduction 4

Unit 1: Sentences and Personal Narrative
Grammar Skills:
Sentences 13
   Blackline Masters 1–3 16
Statements and Questions 19
   Blackline Masters 4–6 22
Commands and Exclamations 25
   Blackline Masters 7–9 28
Subjects and Predicates 31
   Blackline Masters 10–12 34
Vocabulary Skill: Time-Order Words 37
   Blackline Masters 13–14 39
Composition Skill: Main Idea 41
   Blackline Masters 15–16 43
Writing Process: Personal Narrative 45
   Blackline Masters 17–20 49

Unit 2: Nouns and Explanatory Writing
Grammar Skills:
Singular and Plural Nouns 53
   Blackline Masters 21–23 56
Plural Nouns with -*ies* 59
   Blackline Masters 24–26 62
Common and Proper Nouns 65
   Blackline Masters 27–29 68
Singular and Plural Possessive Nouns 71
   Blackline Masters 30–32 74
Vocabulary Skill: Compound Words 77
   Blackline Masters 33–34 79
Composition Skill: Organization 81
   Blackline Masters 35–36 83
Writing Process: Explanatory Writing 85
   Blackline Masters 37–40 89

Unit 3: Verbs and Persuasive Writing
Grammar Skills:
Present-Tense Verbs 93
   Blackline Masters 41–43 96
Subject-Verb Agreement 99
   Blackline Masters 44–46 102
Past-Tense Verbs 105
   Blackline Masters 47–49 108
Future-Tense Verbs 111
   Blackline Masters 50–52 114
Vocabulary Skill: Prefixes 117
   Blackline Masters 53–54 119
Composition Skill: Leads and Endings 121
   Blackline Masters 55–56 123
Writing Process: Persuasive Writing 125
   Blackline Masters 57–60 129

Unit 4: Verbs and Writing that Compares

Grammar Skills:
Main Verbs and Helping Verbs 133
    Blackline Masters 61–63 136
Irregular Verbs 139
    Blackline Masters 64–66 142
Contractions with *Not* 145
    Blackline Masters 67–69 148
Vocabulary Skill: Suffixes 151
    Blackline Masters 70–71 153
Composition Skill: Writing Descriptions 155
    Blackline Masters 72–73 157
Writing Process: Writing that Compares 159
    Blackline Masters 74–77 163

Unit 5: Pronouns and Expository Writing

Grammar Skills:
Subject and Object Pronouns 167
    Blackline Masters 78–80 170
Pronoun-Verb Agreement 173
    Blackline Masters 81–83 176
Possessive Pronouns 179
    Blackline Masters 84–86 182
Vocabulary Skill: Homophones 185
    Blackline Masters 87–88 187
Composition Skill: Outlining 189
    Blackline Masters 89–90 191
Writing Process: Expository Writing 193
    Blackline Masters 91–94 197

Unit 6: Adjectives, Adverbs, and Writing a Story

Grammar Skills:
Adjectives that Tell What Kind 201
    Blackline Masters 95–97 204
Adjectives that Tell How Many 207
    Blackline Masters 98–100 210
Adjectives that Compare 213
    Blackline Masters 101–103 216
Adverbs that Tell How, When, or Where 219
    Blackline Masters 104–106 222
Vocabulary Skill: Synonyms and Antonyms 225
    Blackline Masters 107–108 227
Composition Skill: Beginning, Middle, and End 229
    Blackline Masters 109–110 231
Writing Process: Writing a Story 233
    Blackline Masters 111–114 237

Meeting the Needs of Second-Language Learners with McGraw-Hill Language Arts

McGraw-Hill Language Arts is dedicated to making all students, including second-language learners, effective communicators. The Teacher's Editions at each grade level provide point-of-use suggestions to encourage the participation of second-language learners in each lesson. This Language Support Handbook expands on those suggestions with strategies and activities designed to help you move second-language learners through the stages of language acquisition and prepare them for success in the mainstream language arts curriculum.

Features of the Second-Language Acquisition Program

A language-rich, risk-free setting

The Natural Approach to Language Learning Most people learn to speak fluently by listening, imitating, and trying out a new language. McGraw-Hill Language Arts, through this Language Support Handbook, maximizes this experience by making the classroom a language-rich, risk-free setting where students experiment with language in various contexts. By creating an environment where there is a real need to communicate, the program allows students to produce more language and to make great strides toward fluency.

Whole class instruction around the same theme

Thematic Units The program uses themes to create the context which makes language content meaningful and accessible. In each grade, vocabulary, concepts, and language skills are developed across six themes. Because instruction for the whole class is planned around the same theme or concept, inclusion of and appropriate instruction for second-language learners are ensured.

Meet needs at different levels

Multilevel Strategies Each lesson in this Language Support Handbook provides teaching strategies for students at various proficiency levels. Organized to parallel the mainstream language arts curriculum for each grade level, the multilevel learning activities allow all students access to grade-level content.

Bring out the best in every learner

Variety of Instructional Groupings To bring out the best in all learners, the program uses a variety of instructional groupings: (a) pairs—new English learners are paired with more proficient speakers; (b) small groups—students at all proficiency levels work together; (c) individual interaction with tutors, partners, teaching assistants, and parents; and (d) whole class activities.

Make use of informal assessment opportunities

Appropriate Assessment This Language Support Handbook provides for ongoing evaluation where the processes and products of students' work serve as the basis for assessment. Evaluation strategies include using teacher observations and interactions as a basis for assessment, allowing students to perform an activity that will show the application of a concept, and evaluating progress through student portfolios

Communicating in Every Way

To promote understanding of messages necessary to acquire language, the language support program enables you to cover concepts using a variety of sensory input such as gestures, pictures, graphic organizers, demonstrations, role-plays, pantomime, and variations in pitch and tone of voice. Activities that require total physical response (TPR) are indicated throughout this Language Support Handbook.

Multi-sensory input

Total Physical Response TPR is a well-established and successful technique that links language to a physical response. The classic game of "Simon Says" is a vivid example. The teacher (or a student) can call out a series of commands (i.e., "Simon says, raise your arms") and students respond with the appropriate physical gesture—in this case, by raising their arms. The advantage of this technique is it links language to the "here and now," giving second-language learners, especially at the early stages, a concrete forum for language practice. As your students continue to use TPR and their oral proficiency increases, you will find that they will naturally rely less and less on the technique. Until that point is reached, however, TPR will engage your second-language learners, build their vocabulary, and encourage them to develop and improve the oral language skills they need to master in order to achieve full English proficiency.

Concrete forum for language practice

Examples of Appropriate TPR Commands

Stand up	Giggle	Turn your head to the right
Sit down	Make a face	Drum your fingers
Touch the floor	Flex your muscles	Wet your lips
Raise your arm	Wave to me	Blow a kiss
Put down your arm	Shrug your shoulders	Cough
Pat your cheek	Tickle your side	Sneeze
Wipe your face	Clap your hands	Shout "help"
Scratch your knee	Point to the ceiling	Spell your name
Massage your neck	Cry	Laugh
Stretch	Yawn	Sing
Whisper (a word)	Hum	Hop on one foot
Step forward	Lean backwards	Make a fist
Shake your hand	(Name), walk to the door	(Name), turn on the lights

Source: Richard-Amato, P. (1996). Making it happen: Interaction in the second-language classroom, 2nd ed. White Plains, N.Y.: Addison-Wesley Publishing Group/Longman

Stages of Second-Language Acquisition

Second-language learners move through a series of predictable stages as they make strides toward fluency. The following chart was designed to provide you with a set of reasonable expectations and appropriate teaching approaches to meet the unique needs of students at each language proficiency level.

Stages	Students are able to:	Appropriate teaching approaches include:
1 **Pre-Production**	• understand broad concepts and the gist of conversation • extract meaning from multi-sensory clues such as gestures and visuals • respond non-verbally by drawing and acting out vocabulary, concepts, and events • transfer acquired skills from their first-language learning experience • apply prior knowledge to their current classroom experience • gain greater familiarity with the sounds and patterns of English by listening actively to speakers and audio/video recordings of various contexts	• building on prior knowledge and existing skills developed in the first language • modeling tasks and giving examples • providing opportunities for active listening through dialogue, read-alouds, choral reading, and audio/visual presentations • providing visual support for oral and written messages, such as with realia, manipulatives, and illustrations • allowing students to use total physical response to participate in language activities • encouraging nonverbal expressions, such as mime, art, music, and dance • lavishing praise for all attempts to communicate
2 **Early Production**	• understand much more of what is being said • begin repeating and producing English words, phrases, and simple sentences • understand and use greetings and common expressions with confidence • show some reading comprehension if illustrations are present • demonstrate identification and classification of people, places, and things • begin framing questions to clarify meaning or request more information	• presenting the lesson in the context of students' personal experiences • modeling expected short responses to verbal or written prompts • asking questions that require one- or two-word responses • providing visual support for oral and written messages, such as with realia, manipulatives, and illustrations • providing opportunities for students to create labels and captions for objects and pictures • providing an experiential environment in which students may freely engage in active listening and speaking • encouraging all forms of creative expression such as mime, art, music, and dance • allowing students sufficient time to hear, think, and formulate responses • lavishing praise for every risk taken

Stages	Students are able to:	Appropriate teaching approaches include:
3 **Speech Emergence**	• demonstrate increased comprehension of spoken English • respond in longer phrases or sentences with less hesitation • understand oral and written communication about personal experiences • discuss everyday events, the past, and some future personal events • incorporate content area concepts in oral and written expression • begin to read English without accompanying illustrations • work with less supervision, using previously learned routines	• modeling correct language forms after accepting responses • asking open-ended questions that require short answers and higher-level thinking skills • providing oral and written activities that validate students' cultural identities • using heterogeneous groupings to enable students of different abilities to assist one another (peer tutoring) • providing opportunities for oral and written expression for different purposes and audiences • exposing students to a variety of content-area experiences • gently allowing students silent periods and lapses of decreased correctness as they assimilate new material • lavishing praise for every risk taken
4, 5 **Intermediate and Advanced Fluency**	• understand oral and written communication involving more abstract themes • converse with varied grammatical structures and more extensive vocabulary • express thoughts and feelings with fluency • demonstrate skills in persuading, evaluating, justifying, and elaborating • engage in debates and discuss "what-if" situations • write for different audiences and purposes while demonstrating increased levels of accuracy and correctness • work independently on their own instructional level (At stage 5, students are able to use extensive vocabulary and complex grammatical structures in much the same way as their native English-speaking peers.)	• modeling correct English language patterns and structures after accepting responses • asking open-ended questions that require more detailed answers and higher-level thinking skills • focusing on oral and written communication that requires higher-order language such as persuasion, analysis, and evaluation • allowing students to discuss and model learning strategies • using a variety of instructional groupings to bring out the best in every learner and create opportunities for peer tutoring • integrating language arts and content-area learning experiences • providing opportunities for more abstract oral and written expression for a variety of purposes and audiences

Scope and Sequence

Oral Language Development

All students in grade 3 are expected to:	Teaching approaches to help second language learners at each stage meet expectations include the following:
<ul><li>understand and be able to use complete and correct declarative, interrogative, imperative, and exclamatory sentences in oral communications</li><li>organize ideas chronologically or around major points of information</li><li>respond to questions with appropriate elaboration</li><li>ask thoughtful questions</li><li>retell, paraphrase, and explain what has been said by a speaker</li><li>connect and relate prior experiences, insights, and ideas to those of a speaker</li><li>compare oral traditions that reflect customs, regions, and cultures</li><li>choose and adapt spoken language appropriate to the audience, purpose, and the occasion</li><li>distinguish between the speaker's opinions and verifiable facts</li><li>identify the musical elements of literary language</li><li>read prose and poetry aloud with fluency, rhythm, and pace</li><li>make descriptive presentations that use concrete sensory details</li><li>make narrative and informational presentations</li><li>clarify and enhance oral presentations through the use of appropriate props</li><li>use clear and specific vocabulary to communicate ideas</li><li>plan and present dramatic presentations of experiences, stories, poems, or plays</li><li>compare ideas and points of view expressed in broadcast and print media</li></ul>	**Stage 1: Pre-Production** <ul><li>modeling of verbal prompts by gesturing, role-playing, pantomiming</li><li>pointing to pictures or real objects to demonstrate meanings</li><li>encouraging students to respond in nonverbal ways</li><li>providing a risk-free environment where any kind of speech production is welcomed but not required</li></ul>**Stage 2: Early Production** <ul><li>building on existing oral language skills</li><li>asking *yes/no*, *either/or*, and simple questions that require one- or two-word responses</li><li>simplifying, restating, repeating and demonstrating verbal prompts</li><li>encouraging the use of TPR (Total Physical Response) to demonstrate understanding</li><li>providing activities that allow students to manipulate or label real objects or pictures</li><li>allowing for some participation in paired or small-group speaking and listening activities</li><li>motivating students to take risks with language</li></ul>**Stage 3: Speech Emergence** <ul><li>providing meaningful contexts where students can express themselves orally</li><li>asking open-ended questions that require short responses and higher-level thinking skills</li><li>drawing analogies to students' personal experiences to explain culturally unfamiliar topics</li><li>allowing sufficient time for students to hear, think, and formulate responses</li><li>accepting students' oral responses even if they are not grammatically correct and use unvaried sentence structure</li><li>setting up heterogeneous groups to give modeling of spoken English a natural context</li></ul>**Stages 4 and 5: Intermediate and Advanced Fluency** <ul><li>modeling correct oral language conventions</li><li>asking open-ended questions that require detailed responses and higher-level thinking skills</li><li>creating realistic contexts for debates, discussion of "what-if" situations, and elaboration of ideas</li><li>providing speaking and listening activities that allow students to analyze, compare and contrast, and make generalizations</li><li>assigning the same oral language activities given to the mainstream class, rephrasing and clarifying directions as needed</li></ul>

Language Patterns and Structures

All students in grade 3 are expected to exhibit understanding of:	Teaching approaches to help second language learners at each stage meet expectations include the following:
• Sentences • Statements and Questions • Commands and Exclamations • Subjects and Predicates • Singular and Plural Nouns • Plural Nouns with *-ies* • Common and Proper Nouns • Singular and Plural Possessive Nouns • Present-Tense Verbs • Subject-Verb Agreement • Past-Tense Verbs • Future-Tense Verbs • Main Verbs and Helping Verbs • Irregular Verbs • Contractions with *Not* • Subject and Object Pronouns • Pronoun-Verb Agreement • Possessive Pronouns • Adjectives that Tell What Kind • Adjectives that Tell How Many • Adjectives that Compare • Adverbs that Tell How, When, or Where	**Stage 1: Pre-Production** • clarifying verbal and written prompts by using gestures, role-playing, pantomiming • using realia or manipulatives to demonstrate meanings • encouraging nonverbal responses such as drawing pictures or acting out **Stage 2: Early Production** • using prior language skills as springboards to teach new language patterns • asking *yes/no*, *either/or*, and simple questions that require one- or two-word responses • simplifying, restating, repeating, and demonstrating verbal and written prompts • encouraging the use of TPR (Total Physical Response) to demonstrate understanding • providing activities that allow students to manipulate or label real objects or pictures • allowing for some participation in paired or small-group activities • motivating students to take risks with language **Stage 3: Speech Emergence** • providing meaningful contexts where students can apply language patterns • asking open-ended questions that require short responses and higher-level thinking skills • drawing analogies to students' personal experiences to explain culturally unfamiliar structures and patterns • allowing for silent periods when students internally rehearse new language skills • accepting students' responses even if they are not grammatically correct and use unvaried sentence structure • setting up mixed-ability groups to give modeling of English language structures and patterns a natural context **Stages 4 and 5: Intermediate and Advanced Fluency** • modeling correct English language patterns and structures • asking open-ended questions that require detailed responses and higher-level thinking skills • creating realistic contexts for using correct grammar and sentence structures • providing activities that allow students to use varied grammatical structures and more extensive vocabulary • assigning the same practice exercises given to the mainstream class, rephrasing and clarifying directions as needed

Vocabulary, Composition, and Study Skills

All students in grade 3 are expected to exhibit understanding of skills and concepts in each area.

Teaching approaches to help second language learners at each stage meet expectations include the following:

Vocabulary Skills

- Time-Order Words
- Compound Words
- Prefixes
- Suffixes
- Homophones
- Synonyms and Antonyms

Composition Skills

- Main Idea
- Organization
- Leads and Endings
- Writing Descriptions
- Outlining
- Beginning, Middle, and End

Study Skills

- Conduct an Interview
- Use Parts of a Book
- Note-Taking Using Library Sources
- On-line Search
- Use an Encyclopedia
- Use a Thesaurus

Stage 1: Pre-Production
- showing real objects or large visuals to make academic content comprehensible
- linking sounds to pictures and pictures to sounds
- using gestures, pantomime, or role-playing to demonstrate concepts and tasks
- encouraging nonverbal participation in learning activities
- providing ample opportunities for students to absorb the language-rich environment in the classroom

Stage 2: Early Production
- building on prior knowledge to develop new skills and concepts
- asking questions that require predictable one- or two-word responses
- simplifying, restating, repeating, and demonstrating verbal and written prompts
- encouraging the use of TPR (Total Physical Response) to demonstrate understanding
- providing activities that allow students to manipulate or label real objects or pictures
- allowing for some participation in paired or small-group activities
- motivating students to take risks with new vocabulary and strategies

Stage 3: Speech Emergence
- providing meaningful contexts where students can apply vocabulary, composition, and study skills
- asking open-ended questions that require short responses and higher-level thinking skills
- drawing analogies to students' personal experiences to explain culturally unfamiliar content
- allowing sufficient time for students to hear, think, and formulate responses
- setting up heterogeneous groups to enable students to learn from their peers

Stages 4 and 5: Intermediate and Advanced Fluency
- modeling correct use of new vocabulary, composition, or study skills
- asking open-ended questions that require detailed responses and higher-level thinking skills
- providing activities that allow students to use more extensive vocabulary
- creating realistic contexts for using reference materials
- assigning the same practice exercises given to the mainstream class, rephrasing and clarifying directions as needed

Scope and Sequence

Writing

All students in grade 3 are expected to:	Teaching approaches to help second language learners at each stage meet expectations include the following:

• **write for a different purpose/audience**
  • write to inform
  • write to explain
  • write to entertain
  • write to persuade
  • write to express, discover, record, reflect on ideas, and problem solve
 	
• **write in different modes**
  • personal narrative
  • explanatory writing
  • persuasive writing
  • writing that compares
  • expository writing
  • story writing
 	
• **write using a variety of forms**
  • questions, jokes, riddles, rules, book titles, outlines, shopping lists, supply lists, paragraphs, how-to paragraphs, notes, messages, conversations, summaries, descriptions, directions, bumper stickers, character sketches, book jackets, signs, reviews, friendly and business letters, thank-you letters, invitations, news or magazine articles, news reports, weather forecasts, book reports, diary entries, comic strips, posters, postcards, journal entries, instructions, photo essays, short stories, poems, songs, captions, advertisements
 	
• **apply writing processes**
  • prewriting
  • research and inquiry
  • drafting
  • revising
  • proofreading
  • publishing
	Stage 1: Pre-Production
	• modeling of tasks by gesturing, role-playing, pantomiming
	• using pictures or real objects to demonstrate meanings
	• encouraging students to respond in nonverbal ways
	• creating a risk-free setting where any kind of written production is welcomed but not required
	
	Stage 2: Early Production
	• building on existing writing skills
	• simplifying, restating, repeating and demonstrating writing prompts
	• using appropriate TPR (Total Physical Response) commands to provide a concrete forum for language practice
	• encourage language production while students manipulate or label real objects or pictures
	• allowing for some participation in paired or small-group writing activities
	• motivating students to take risks with writing
	
	Stage 3: Speech Emergence
	• providing meaningful contexts where students can express themselves in writing
	• requiring short written responses using higher-level thinking skills
	• drawing analogies to students' personal experiences to explain culturally unfamiliar topics
	• allowing sufficient time for students to hear, think, and formulate written compositions
	• setting up heterogeneous groups to allow students to learn from one another
	
	Stages 4 and 5: Intermediate and Advanced Fluency
	• modeling correct English writing conventions
	• creating realistic contexts for written communication
	• providing writing activities that allow students to narrate, explain, persuade, analyze, compare and contrast, and make generalizations
	• encouraging active participation in mainstream learning activities

Addressing Specific Problems

A student at the pre-production level seems withdrawn and won't say a word.

Students at the pre-production stage of language acquisition normally go through a silent period during which they are internally transferring learned skills from their first language and prior academic experience. They are absorbing the language-rich environment of your classroom.

A student at the early production level is often hesitant to speak in class.

If silence is habitual, it might be a result of lack of self-confidence or an issue about risk-taking or appropriateness. Many factors, such as culture, gender, personality, and personal experience, influence an individual's perception of acceptable risk or appropriateness. Provide a risk-free environment in which participation is welcomed but not mandated.

A student at the speech emergence level is suddenly hesitant to participate and makes careless grammatical errors when he or she does answer.

Brief silent periods often signal that new vocabulary and language patterns are being internally rehearsed and learned. Resume oral prompts with volunteers while you wait for the student to either volunteer an answer or request clarification. If, when the student does speak, his or her grammar isn't perfect, that is understandable. Focus instead on whether the new material is being assimilated correctly and commend him or her for a job well done.

A new student has trouble transitioning from drawing to writing text for written assignments and also has difficulty reading.

Consider the differences between English and the student's first language. Does it use a different alphabet? Is the text read from left to right or from right to left? Naturally, reading and writing a completely different language takes a great deal of patience and encouragement.

A student who has no trouble with conversational English demonstrates below-average performance in academic contexts.

Academic language proficiency develops much later, often not until the fourth or fifth stage of language acquisition is achieved. To help students make giant strides toward fluency, provide comprehensible materials connected to the themes of the mainstream curriculum.

Some students can't seem to give a straight answer. Some never ask questions.

Cultural backgrounds often come into play during classroom interactions. For instance, in some Asian cultures it is considered more polite to communicate thoughts indirectly than to be bluntly direct. In some Hispanic cultures, questioning may be viewed as disrespectful behavior as it interrupts the teacher's presentation. Be careful not to ask students to choose between the home culture and the dominant culture in the classroom. Let them observe how classmates communicate, and give them time to assimilate your preferred model for communication.

Students exhibit mixed skills, such as the oral skills of Advanced Fluency, the reading skills of Intermediate Fluency, and the writing skills of Speech Emergence.

Second-language learners tend to exhibit ever-changing proficiency levels in listening, speaking, reading, and writing. Build on their strengths to improve on their weaknesses.

I. DEVELOP ORAL LANGUAGE
Oral Focus on Grammar Skill

Objective: Orally describe pictures and tell what happens in them in complete sentences.

TPR

Whole Group Oral Language Activity

Ask students to look at the photograph on page 2 of the textbook. Ask: *Who is in the picture?* Write their answers on the chalkboard. Ask: *What is she doing?* Write their answers on the chalkboard.

Tell students that in order to be a sentence, a group of words must tell two things. It must name the person or thing being talked about, and it must tell what happens. Ask a volunteer to point to a word that tells *who* on the chalkboard. Ask another volunteer to point to the words that tell what happens in the picture. Model making a sentence out of the words, one that tells *who* and *what happens.* Then write it on the chalkboard and point out the capital letter that begins the sentence.

Repeat the activity with the photograph on page 3.

Scaffolded Verbal Prompting

Use the following verbal prompts to help students better understand complete sentences.

Nonverbal Prompt for Active Participation

Pre-Production: *Look at the picture. Point to a person. Imitate or show what that person is doing.*

One- or Two-Word Response Prompt

Early Production: *Name a person in the picture. Tell what that person might do.*

Prompt for Short Answers to Higher-Level Thinking Skills

Speech Emergence: *Tell me who is in the picture. What is that person doing? Which words did you use to tell what that person is doing?*

Prompt for Detailed Answers to Higher-Level Thinking Skills

Intermediate and Advanced Fluency: *In one sentence, tell who is in the picture and what she is doing. Did you use a complete sentence? Does it tell who it is about and what happened?*

II. DEVELOP GRAMMAR SKILLS IN CONTEXT
Visual/Physical Focus on Grammar Skill

Objective: Develop and demonstrate an understanding of what makes a sentence complete.

Blackline Master 1

[**Answer:** The sentence is about Rob.]

TPR

Extension: Write sentences children make up on the chalkboard. As you read each one aloud, ask volunteers to substitute their own name as the "who" in the sentence, repeating it aloud.

Extension: Have partners work together to make complete sentences out of the cards they both hold. Ask them to share the sentences by reading them aloud.

Whole Group Activity

Write a complete sentence on the chalkboard: *Mike picked up a shell.* Draw a circle around the word *Mike,* explaining that it tells who the sentence is about. Draw a line under the rest of the sentence. Explain that this part tells what happens.

Provide students with a copy of Blackline Master 1, scissors, and glue. Read it aloud with them, and ask them to point to the name of the person the sentence is about. Have them cut out the picture that matches this subject and paste it in the blank box. Then have them write the name of the person on the line under the picture.

Small Group Activity

Ask students to think of things they've done with their families. *(We went to the zoo. We visited my uncle. We swam in a pool.)* Invite volunteers to act out one of these things, then tell about it in a sentence. Ask: *Who (swam in a pool)?* and *What did ____ do?*

Partner Activity

Make ten cards labeled with the name of a person or thing *(e.g., Bobby, girl, cat),* and ten that tell an action *(ate a pizza, went to bed, sang a song).* Shuffle the cards, and have each partner take six. Each partner should then try to combine his or her cards into a pair including one card that tells *who* or *what,* and one that tells *what happened.* Help partners to see that combining any two cards do not necessarily make a sentence; there needs to be one *who* card and one *what* card to make sense.

Technology Link

Have partners challenge each other to write complete sentences. Each types a *who* or *what* and a *what happened* word(s) into a word processing program. The partner must add words to turn them into a complete sentence. Remind them to capitalize the first word and place a period at the end of each sentence.

III. PRACTICE GRAMMAR SKILLS
Written Focus on Grammar Skills

Use the following Blackline Masters to reinforce grammar skills.

Introduce Blackline Master 2: Ama At the Beach

Explain that sentences that are not complete are called *fragments.* In order for a sentence to be complete, it has to tell who or what the sentence is about. It also has to tell what happens. Distribute Blackline Master 2. Read the directions aloud with students. Explain that each of the sentences is incomplete. It is missing a word in the part of the sentence that tells what happens. Guide students to cut out the pictures and place them in the boxes of the incomplete sentences. Share them aloud, and discuss whether each one is now a complete sentence.

Objective: Form complete sentences from fragments by adding a picture to stand for a word.

Materials: Blackline Master 2; scissors; glue or paste

[**Answers:** 1. seashell, 2. sand pail, 3. sandwich]

Informal Assessment

Have students turn back to page 3 and read sentence 12 in More Practice A. Then read it without the last two words. "People enjoy…" Ask students to add a word or words to make complete sentences.

Introduce Blackline Master 3: Is It a Sentence?

Pair students of varying language levels. Distribute Blackline Master 3. Read the directions aloud with students. Then have partners read the sentences aloud together and discuss whether each is a complete sentence. Have students work independently to add words to the incomplete sentences. Then have them compare what they wrote with their partner.

Objective: Identify complete sentences, and make complete sentences out of fragments.

Materials: Blackline Master 3

[**Answers:** 1. yes, 2. yes, 3. no, 4. no, 5. no. Sentences for items 3, 4, and 5 will vary.]

Informal Assessment

Have students turn to page 3 and look at the picture of the girl holding the starfish. Ask them to make up a sentence that tells what is happening in the picture. Is it a complete sentence?

Use the following chart to assess and reteach:

Are students able to: orally tell about a picture?	Reteach using oral warm-up on TE page 1G, simplifying the prompts as needed.
tell who or what the sentence is about and what happens?	Reteach using the Language Support Activity on TE page 2.
recognize a complete sentence?	Reteach using the Reteach Activity on TE page 3.

At the Beach

Rob went to the beach.
Which picture tells who the sentence is about? Cut it out and paste it here:

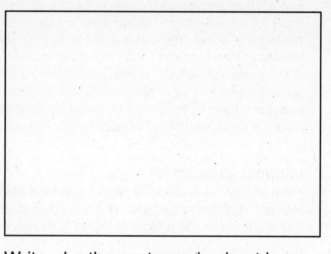

Write who the sentence is about here:

_____

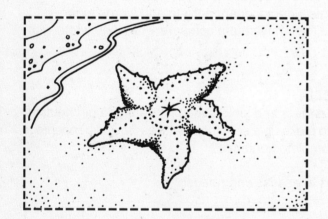

Ama at the Beach

Cut out the pictures at the bottom of the page.
Paste a picture in each box to finish the sentences.

1. Ama picked up a 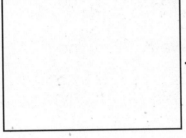 .

2. She put it in her 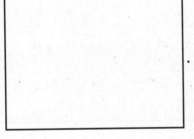 .

3. Ama ate her  .

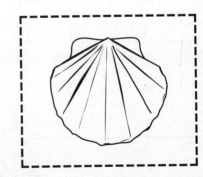

Is It a Sentence?

Read each item. Is it a complete sentence? Circle *yes* or *no*. If it is not complete, write it on the lines below and add words or draw pictures to complete it.

1. Tim and I saw some fish.   yes   no

2. Dave swam.   yes   no

3. My sea shells.   yes   no

4. Was hot.   yes   no

5. The sun.   yes   no

_____

_____

_____

_____

_____

STATEMENTS AND QUESTIONS

I. DEVELOP ORAL LANGUAGE
Oral Focus on Grammar Skill

Objective: Identify statements and questions.

Whole Group Oral Language Activity

Write the words *statement* and *question* on the chalkboard. Invite students to look at the picture of butterflies on page 4. Point to one of the butterflies. Ask: *Tell me something about this butterfly*. Write the student's response on the chalkboard next to the word *statement*. Explain that a sentence that tells something is a statement. It ends with a period. Tell students to ask something they would like to learn about the butterfly. Write questions they ask on the chalkboard next to the word *question*. Explain that a question is a sentence that asks something. It ends with a question mark.

Scaffolded Verbal Prompting

Use the following verbal prompts to help students better understand statements and questions.

Nonverbal Prompt for Active Participation

Pre-Production: *Point to one of the butterflies pictured on page 4. Act out this question: How does a butterfly eat?*

One- or Two-Word Response Prompt

Early Production: *Point to one of the butterflies pictured on page 4. Tell what color it is.*

Prompt for Short Answers to Higher-Level Thinking Skills

Speech Emergence: *Tell something that a butterfly on page 4 is doing. Ask a question about what one of them is doing.*

Prompt for Detailed Answers to Higher-Level Thinking Skills

Intermediate and Advanced Fluency: *In a sentence that is a statement, tell something about one of the butterflies on page 4. In a sentence that is a question, ask something you would like to learn about one of the butterflies.*

II. DEVELOP GRAMMAR SKILLS IN CONTEXT
Visual/Physical Focus on Grammar Skill

Objective: Identify sentences that are statements and questions.

Blackline Master 4

TPR

Whole Group Activity

Write two sentences on the chalkboard, one labeled *Statement* and one labeled *Question,* for example: *Butterflies come in many colors. What is your favorite color?* Point out the period at the end of the statement and the question mark at the end of the question. Provide each student with a copy of Blackline Master 4. Tell students to use crayons or markers to color the Statement card blue and the Question card yellow. Then have them cut out each card. Ask them to hold up the Statement card when you read a sentence that is a statement and the Question card when you read a sentence that is a question. Read several sentences of your own choosing, or use the ones on pages 4 and 5 of the students' textbook.

Extension: Write two statements and two questions on the chalkboard, <u>without</u> end punctuation. Invite students to identify them as either statements or questions and to add the correct end punctuation.

Small Group Activity

Ask students to think of a meal time at home. What do different family members do? *(My brother Sam sets the table. I take the dishes to the sink. My baby sister makes a mess.)* Ask groups to act out the sentences that describe what people do at meal time. As a student acts out a sentence, ask that student or another one to say what is happening in a sentence. Then ask students to turn one of these statements into a question. Example: *Who washes the dishes?*

Extension: Have partners make sentence strips of their questions and answers, choosing a different color paper for questions and for answers. Allow students time to display the sentence strips and read them aloud.

Partner Activity

Have partners work together to write five questions. Then have them write statements that answer each question. (Examples: *What color butterfly did you see? That butterfly is yellow.*) Have students practice "interviewing" each other: one asks the question and one answers it with the sentences students have made up.

Technology Link

Type three questions into a word processing program. Have partners work together to answer these questions with statements. Have them type them in underneath the questions. Ask them to read aloud the sentence pairs they have made.

III. PRACTICE GRAMMAR SKILLS
Written Focus on Grammar Skills

Use the following Blackline Masters to reinforce grammar skills.

Introduce Blackline Master 5: Questions and Answers

Objective: Identify statements and questions.

Materials: Blackline Master 5

[**Answers:** 1. S, 2. S, 3. Q, 4. S, 5. Q]

Distribute Blackline Master 5. Read aloud and discuss the directions with students. Discuss what makes a sentence a statement and what makes a sentence a question. Have students mark the sentences with an **S** or a **Q.** Have pairs of students compare their answers.

Informal Assessment

Have students turn to page 5 in their textbooks. Point to sentences 9 and 10 in More Practice A. Ask them to identify each as a question or a statement and explain how they could tell.

Introduce Blackline Master 6: Which One Is It?

Objective: Identify statements and questions and write both of these kinds of sentences.

Materials: Blackline Master 6

[**Answers:** Students should write statements for Box 1 and Box 4 and questions for Box 2 and Box 3]

Distribute Blackline Master 6, and read the directions with students. Discuss what makes a sentence a question and what makes a sentence a statement. Tell students that whatever they decide each sentence is, they will write the other.

Allow students time to read the questions and answers that they write.

Informal Assessment

Ask students to turn to page 5 in their textbooks. What do they see in the picture? Ask them to write a statement about the picture. Then ask them to write a question about it.

Use the following chart to assess and reteach:

Are students able to:	
identify questions and statements?	Reteach using the Language Support Activity on TE page 4.
tell what makes a sentence a statement or a question?	Reteach using the Review the Rules box on page 4.
write a statement and a question?	Reteach using the Reteach Activity on TE page 5.

Statement

Question

Questions and Answers

Look at the sentences. If a sentence is a statement, write **S** on the line next to it. If it is a question, write **Q** on the line next to it.

_____ **1.** Butterflies like red flowers.

_____ **2.** They can see them.

_____ **3.** Can they see yellow ones?

_____ **4.** I don't know.

_____ **5.** Do you want to find out?

Which One Is It?

Read the sentence in each box. If it is a question, write a statement that answers it. If it is a statement, write a question about it.

Are butterflies bugs? _____ _____ _____	That one is black and orange. _____ _____ _____
It is a Monarch butterfly. _____ _____ _____	Have you ever seen one? _____ _____ _____

I. DEVELOP ORAL LANGUAGE
Oral Focus on Grammar Skill

Objective Identify commands and exclamations.

Whole Group Oral Language Activity

Write the words *command* and *exclamation* on the chalkboard. Invite students to look at the picture of the two people on page 7. Ask students to point to the man in the picture. Ask: *What do you think the man might be telling the boy to do?* Write the student's responses on the chalkboard next to the word *command*. Explain that a sentence that tells or asks someone to do something is a command. It ends with a period. Ask students to look at the boy in the picture. Ask: *If he was excited about what he saw through the binoculars, what might the boy say? How would he say it?* Write students' answers on the chalkboard next to the word *exclamation*. Explain that an exclamation is a sentence that shows strong feeling. It ends with an exclamation mark.

Scaffolded Verbal Prompting

Use the following verbal prompts to help students better understand commands and exclamations.

Nonverbal Prompt for Active Participation

Pre-Production: *Point to the person in the picture on page 7 who might be giving a command. Show me what he is doing.*

One- or Two-Word Response Prompt

Early Production: *Point to the train pictured on page 6. Tell something about this train that shows strong feeling.*

Prompt for Short Answers to Higher-Level Thinking Skills

Speech Emergence: *Tell something the conductor of the train on page 6 might tell the passengers to do.*

Prompt for Detailed Answers to Higher-Level Thinking Skills

Intermediate and Advanced Fluency: *In a sentence that is a command, tell what the man in the picture on page 7 might be telling the boy to do. In a sentence that is an exclamation, tell something the boy might say about what he sees through the binoculars.*

II. DEVELOP GRAMMAR SKILLS IN CONTEXT
Visual/Physical Focus on Grammar Skill

Objective: Identify sentences that are commands and exclamations.

Blackline Master 7

TPR

Extension: Write a command and an exclamation on the chalkboard, but put no period or exclamation mark at the ends. Ask for volunteers to come up, point out the command, and add the correct punctuation. Repeat with the exclamation.

Extension: Have partners think of exclamations that might go with each of the safety rules. For example, if the rule was the above *Don't feed the animals,* the exclamation might be: *Here comes the lion!*

Whole Group Activity

Write two sentences on the chalkboard, one labeled *Command* and one labeled *Exclamation.* For example: *Please get off the train. Those wild animals are neat!* Point out the period at the end of the command and the exclamation mark at the end of the exclamation. Provide each student with a copy of Blackline Master 7. Tell students to use crayons or markers to color the Command card green and the Exclamation card pink. Then have them cut out each card. Ask students to hold up the Command card when you read a sentence that is a command, and the Exclamation card when you read a sentence that is an exclamation. Read several sentences of your own choosing, or use the ones on pages 6 and 7 of the students' textbook.

Small Group Activity

Ask students to think about some of the things they did and saw on their way to school this morning. Have them act out a person giving a command. (Example: a crossing guard putting up a hand to tell cars to stop.) Then have them act out the part of someone being excited. As students act out these things, have them tell in words what each person might be saying.

Partner Activity

Have partners work together to come up with a list of safety rules for a particular place or activity. Point out that most safety rules come in the form of a command. Example: *Don't feed the animals.* Have partners share their safety rules with the group.

Technology Link

Have students work together to make a sign or poster, using a computer program—either a word processing program or an art program that allows you to make signs. The sign should include three commands and three exclamations that give details about an event at school, such as a bake sale, a school fair, and so on.

III. PRACTICE GRAMMAR SKILLS
Written Focus on Grammar Skills

Use the following Blackline Masters to reinforce grammar skills.

Introduce Blackline Master 8: Commands and Exclamations

Objective: Identify commands and exclamations and punctuate them correctly.

Materials: Blackline Master 8

[Answers: 1. E; ! 2. C; . 3. C; . 4. E; ! 5. C; .]

Distribute Blackline Master 8. Read aloud and discuss the directions with students. Discuss what makes a sentence a command and what makes a sentence an exclamation. Have students mark the sentences with a **C** or an **E** and circle the correct end mark. Have pairs of students compare their answers.

Informal Assessment

Have students turn to page 7 in their textbooks. Read aloud sentence 9 of More Practice A. Ask, *Is this sentence a command or an exclamation? How do you know?* Repeat the questioning with sentence 10.

Introduce Blackline Master 9: What's Happening?

Objective: Write sentences that give a command or an exclamation.

Materials: Blackline Master 9

[Possible Answers: 1. This race car is fast! 2. Wait for the light to turn green. 3. What a big mountain! 4. Sit next to the chair.]

Distribute Blackline Master 9, and read the directions with students. Go over the first exercise, which has been filled in. Discuss what makes a sentence a command and what makes a sentence an exclamation. Allow time for students to share the commands and exclamations they wrote.

Informal Assessment

Show students a picture of a school event or any other picture that clearly shows people doing something. Ask them to write a sentence that is either a command or an exclamation that is related to the picture.

Use the following chart to assess and reteach:

Are students able to:	
identify commands and exclamations?	Reteach using the Language Support Activity on TE page 6.
tell what makes a sentence a command or an exclamation?	Reteach using the Language Support Activity on TE page 8.
write and correctly punctuate a command and an exclamation?	Reteach using the Reteach Activity on TE page 7.

Command

Exclamation

Commands and Exclamations

Look at the sentences. If a sentence is a command, write **C** on the line next to it and circle the period. If it is an exclamation, write **E** on the line next to it and circle the exclamation mark.

_____ **1.** Wow, this train is so fast   .   !

_____ **2.** Please sit down in your seat   .   !

_____ **3.** Don't eat in here   .   !

_____ **4.** My sister is so bossy   .   !

_____ **5.** Tell me where you're going   .   !

What's Happening?

Look at each picture. Write a sentence about each one in the box next to it. Each sentence should be a command or an exclamation. The first one has been done for you.

This race car
is fast!

I. DEVELOP ORAL LANGUAGE
Oral Focus on Grammar Skill

Objective: Identify subjects and predicates in sentences.

Whole Group Oral Language Activity

Invite students to look at the picture of the dogsled on page 12. Write the words *Subject* and *Predicate* on the chalkboard. Ask: *Point to someone in the picture.* <u>*Who*</u> *is in the picture?* <u>*Who*</u> *else is in the picture? Point to something in the picture.* <u>*What*</u> *is in the picture?* Write the students' answers under the word *Subject.* Ask: *What is the driver* <u>*doing*</u> *in the picture? What are the dogs* <u>*doing*</u> *in the picture?* Write their answers under the word *Predicate.*

Tell students that every sentence has two main parts—a subject and a predicate. Explain that the subject tells *whom* or *what* the sentence is about. Ask a volunteer to point to or name a "who" or "what" in the picture, such as *the driver.* Then tell them that the predicate is the part of the sentence that tells what the subject *does* or *is.* Ask a volunteer to tell what the driver is doing. *(steers, pushes, drives)* Next, provide a subject such as, *The driver* or *The dogs* and ask students to add a predicate related to the picture to form a complete sentence. For example: *The driver is steering* or *The dogs are pulling.*

Scaffolded Verbal Prompting

Use the following verbal prompts to help students better understand subjects and predicates.

Nonverbal Prompt for Active Participation

Pre-Production: *Look at the picture on page 12. Point to a person. Then show what that person is doing.*

One- or Two-Word Response Prompt

Early Production: *Point to the picture on page 12. Name a person in the picture. Tell something that person might do.*

Prompt for Short Answers to Higher-Level Thinking Skills

Speech Emergence: *Tell me who is in the picture on page 12. What is the person doing? What words tell what the person is doing?*

Prompt for Detailed Answers to Higher-Level Thinking Skills

Intermediate and Advanced Fluency: *Tell me in one sentence who the person is and what the person is doing. Repeat the sentence. Tell which words are the subject? Which words are the predicate?*

II. DEVELOP GRAMMAR SKILLS IN CONTEXT
Visual/Physical Focus on Grammar Skill

Objective: Develop and demonstrate an understanding of subjects and predicates.

Blackline Master 10

TPR

Extension: Write two sentences on the chalkboard. Ask volunteers to make one line under the subject and two lines under the predicate.

Sara is in the play.

The lead dog is the strongest.

Extension: Deal out the remaining subject and predicate cards. Instead of combining two cards to make a sentence, have students think of a new subject to add to the predicate shown on the predicate cards and a new predicate to add to the subject shown on the subject cards. Invite students to read their complete sentences aloud.

Whole Group Activity

Write a sentence on the chalkboard such as *The dogs pull the sled.* Draw one line under the subject and two lines under the predicate. Distribute Blackline Master 10 to each student. Give them time to color the S (for subject) red and the P (for predicate) blue. Tell them to cut out the letter shapes. Then invite students to hold up the S card when they hear you read aloud the subject of a sentence and the P card when they hear the predicate. Choose sentences from the student textbook, pages 12–15, or use sentences of your own.

Small Group Activity

Ask students to think about something they did yesterday. *(Jenna played baseball. Tim went to the zoo. Sara made a cake.)* Ask group members to take turns acting out the sentences. As each sentence is acted out, invite a student to say it aloud. Ask another volunteer to name the subject and the predicate of each sentence.

Partner Activity

Write ten sentences that tell about something students might do. *(I joined the Boy Scouts. I ate a pizza. I go to school.)* Use these sentences to make a deck of subject and predicate cards for each pair of students. Shuffle the cards and deal out five cards to each student. Have students make complete sentences by combining a subject card and a predicate card. Then have students read their sentences aloud.

Technology Link

Create the subject/predicate card activity above on the computer. Type in ten subjects below the heading "Subject" and ten predicates below the heading "Predicate." Have students use the computer's cut and paste features to mix and match the subjects and predicates into new complete sentences.

III. PRACTICE GRAMMAR SKILLS
Written Focus on Grammar Skills

Use the following Blackline Masters to reinforce grammar skills.

Objective: Form complete sentences from subjects and predicates.

Materials: Blackline Master 11; scissors; paste or glue

[**Answers:** 1. The cat slept on the chair. 2. Kara is swimming. 3. The airplane soared into the sky. 4. Everyone ate pizza. 5. Sam is writing a letter.]

Introduce Blackline Master 11: Find the Subject/Predicate
Distribute Blackline Master 11. Read aloud and discuss the directions with students. Have students cut out the pictures at the bottom of the page and paste each next to the sentence it shows. Then have students read the sentences aloud, substituting a new subject in each.

Informal Assessment
Have students turn to page 14 in their textbooks. Read aloud Guided Practice sentences 2 and 3. Ask students to identify the subject and the predicate in each sentence.

Objective: Complete sentences by adding either a subject or a predicate.

Materials: Blackline Master 12

[**Possible Answers:**
1. The children put on a play.
2. Liam read his lines.
3. Then he put on his mask.
4. Maria didn't want to be in the play. 5. The teacher said she didn't have to be in it.
6. We all had fun!]

Introduce Blackline Master 12: Add a Subject/Predicate
Distribute Blackline Master 12. Read aloud and discuss the directions with students, and go over the sample item that has been done for them. Remind students that their answers will differ because they are made to be filled in by each student according to his or her own ideas. Encourage students to read their completed sentences aloud.

Informal Assessment
Have students turn to page 15 in their textbooks. Ask them to write a complete sentence that tells something about the picture of the children in masks on that page. Have students underline the subject of their sentence once and the predicate twice.

Use the following chart to assess and reteach:

Are students able to:	
orally tell what they see in a picture?	Reteach using the Language Support Activity on TE page 12.
put together subjects and predicates to make complete sentences?	Reteach using the Language Support Activity on TE page 14.
identify the subject and predicate of a sentence?	Reteach using the Reteach Activity on TE page 13.

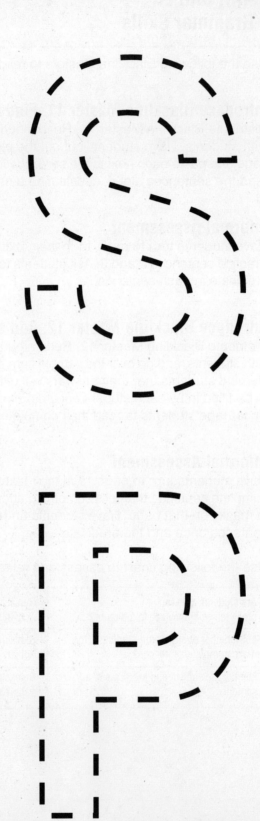

Find the Subject/Predicate

Read each sentence. Circle the subject and underline the predicate. At the bottom of the page, find the picture that shows the sentence. Cut out the picture and paste it in the box next to the sentence.

1. The cat slept on the chair.

2. Kara is swimming.

3. The airplane soared into the sky.

4. Everyone ate pizza.

5. Sam is writing a letter.

Add a Subject/Predicate

Read each sentence. Decide whether the subject or the predicate is missing.
Add that part to the sentence. The first one has been done for you.

1. _____ The children _____ put on a play.

2. Liam _____.

3. Then he _____.

4. _____ didn't want to be in the play.

5. _____ said he didn't have to be in it.

6. We all _____!

TIME-ORDER WORDS

Introduce this lesson before Pupil Edition pages 32–33.

I. DEVELOP ORAL LANGUAGE
Oral Focus on Vocabulary Skill

Objective: Orally describe an adventure using time-order words.

Whole Group Oral Language Activity

Write these words and phrases on separate pieces of drawing paper: *Yesterday, Last Week, Last year, First, Next, Then, After a while,* and *Finally.* Display the words on a chalkledge or pocket chart. Ask volunteers to read the words and then have students read them aloud together. Discuss with students what these words all have in common. *(They all tell about time.)* Explain that speakers and writers use time-order words to make the order in which things happen clear.

Tell students to use the time-order words as they tell about an adventure they have had or would like to have. Model using time-order words in your own adventure story. Point to the time-order words as you say them. For example, say: *Last week I rode on a train to the city. First I bought a ticket. Then I got on the train and sat down. After a while the train pulled out of the station. Next the conductor punched my ticket. Finally we pulled into the city and I got off the train.*

Ask volunteers to tell about their own adventures. Have a partner point to each time-order word as the storyteller says it. Record any new time-order words that students use and add them to the ones on display. Review the words and the way in which they were used in the story.

Scaffolded Verbal Prompting

Use the following verbal prompts to help students better understand how time-order words might help a listener or reader understand the order in which events happen.

Nonverbal Prompt for Active Participation

Pre-Production: *Act out your adventure story. Point to an appropriate time-order word before you show us each part of your story.*

One- or Two-Word Response Prompt

Early Production: *Listen to these three time-order words: finally, first, next. Say the words in their correct order to show when things happen. (first, next, finally)*

Prompt for Short Answers to HIgher-Level Thinking Skills

Speech Emergence: *Name three time-order words that you use at the beginning of a story. (Possible answers: First, Long ago, Today) Name three time-order words you use at the end of a story. (Finally, At Last, Later)*

Prompt for Detailed Answers to Higher-Level Thinking Skills

Intermediate and Advanced Fluency: *Tell the class about what you have done so far today. Use time-order words as you tell about your day. Snap your fingers each time you say a time-order word.*

II. DEVELOP VOCABULARY SKILLS IN CONTEXT
Visual/Physical Focus on Vocabulary Skill

Objective: Describe an experience using time-order words.

Small Group Activity

As a group, discuss a trip that you would like the class to take. Give a time-order word paper to each person in the group. Have each person tell about his/her part of the story.

Partner Activity

Have partners narrate the story of a trip, using time-order words, while the other mimes the action.

TPR

Technology Link

Invite pairs to use a word processing program to write the script for the narrator. Show students how to double-space the text.

III. PRACTICE VOCABULARY SKILLS
Written Focus on Vocabulary Skill

Objective: Identify time-order words that correspond to the order of the story

Materials: Blackline Master 13; pencils

[**Answers:** 1: First; 2: Then; 3: Next; 4: Finally]

Objective: Identify, order and use time-order words to sequence a story.

Materials: Blackline Master 14; scissors, paste or glue

[**Answers:** First: in line for check-in; Second: getting on the plane; Then: flying in a plane; Finally: getting off the plane.]

Introduce Blackline Master 13: Time-Order Match Up

Distribute Blackline Master 13. Read the first sentence with students. Have students choose the correct time-order word to complete this part of the story. Then have students complete the rest of the exercises independently.

Introduce Blackline Master 14: Story Order

Distribute Blackline Master 14. Read aloud the directions. Have children point to where this first picture belongs. Have students complete the page independently.

Informal Assessment

Have students turn to page 33 in the textbook. Refer them to exercise one in Practice A. Ask: *Which word in the sentence tells when the family moved to a new town?* Next, read aloud exercise 6 in Practice B. Ask: *How do you know that the answer is not "next week"? (Next week tells what will happen later. They already went to the zoo.)*

Use the following chart to assess and reteach.

Are students able to: use time-order words correctly in a sequence?	Reteach by using the Language Support Activity on TE page 32
name time-order words that describe a sequence?	Reteach by using the Reteach Activity on TE page 33.

Name _____ Date _____

Time-Order Match Up

Look at the pictures. They tell a story. Read each sentence. Circle the word that correctly completes each sentence. Write the word you circled on the line.

1. _____ we planned our trip.

     Then   First

2. _____ we packed our bags.

     Then   First

3. _____ we put the bags in the car.

     Next   Last

4. _____ we are on our way.

     First   Finally

Story Order

Read the time-order words at the bottom of the page. Cut out the words and put them in order. Paste them in the boxes. Look at the pictures. Cut them out and place them in the boxes.

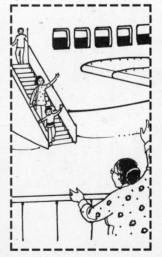

| Second | Then | First | Finally |

MAIN IDEA

Introduce this lesson before Pupil Edition pages 34–35.

I. DEVELOP ORAL LANGUAGE
Oral Focus on Composition Skill

Objective: Orally describe a picture and determine the main idea.
TPR

Extension: Ask students how the girl's narrative would change if she were holding a basketball rather than a surfboard. Have them give a sample Main Idea sentence.

Nonverbal Prompt for Active Participation

One- or Two-Word Response Prompt

Prompt for Short Answers to Higher-Level Thinking Skills

Prompt for Detailed Answers to Higher-Level Thinking Skills

Whole Group Oral Language Activity
Ask students to look at the photograph on page 35. Ask them what they see in the photo. *What is the girl doing? Where might she be?* Explain that this picture could give a personal narrative about an experience the girl had at the beach. Have students pantomime something the girl might do at the beach. Then ask them: *What would be the main idea of the girl's personal narrative about her day at the beach?*

Scaffolded Verbal Prompting
Use the following verbal prompts to help students better determine the main idea.

Pre-Production: *Look at the picture. Imagine that you were with the girl. Show me what you might be doing.*

Early Production: *Tell me one thing in the picture that gives a clue about what the girl is doing and where she is.*

Speech Emergence: *Tell me in a sentence what the girl is doing in the picture.*

Intermediate Fluency: *Imagine that you were telling about the girl's experience in this picture. What would be your main idea? What details would you add to support this main idea?*

II. DEVELOP COMPOSITION SKILLS IN CONTEXT
Visual/Physical Focus on Composition Skill

Objective: Use drawings to show the main idea.

Small Group Activity
Form students into small groups. Have each group choose a main idea topic from a box of slips on which you have written such topics as Going Fishing, Acting in a Play, Playing in a Band, or Shopping for Food. Give students time to work on a drawing together that shows the main idea. Then have each group present their main idea drawing to the other groups. Groups should try to guess each other's main idea from the drawings. If the drawings do not suggest the main idea, have the groups brainstorm for details they might add to make the main idea clearer.

Partner Activity

Extension: Have pairs turn their main idea and supporting details into sentences that make up a paragraph. Have them post their narratives with the picture on the bulletin board.

Cut out a selection of pictures from magazines. Give one to each pair of students. Ask students to think about the subject of the picture and to write a main idea sentence about it. Then have each member of the pair think of two details they could add about the picture.

Technology Link

Have each group make up a narrative to go along with their drawing. Ask them to type the sentences into a word processing program. Then allow time for other groups to read and critique the narratives. Have students make corrections and improvements to their narratives on the computer, using suggestions from other groups.

III. PRACTICE COMPOSITION SKILLS
Written Focus on Composition Skill

Objective: Identify the main idea.

Materials: Blackline Master 15

[Answers: (Possible responses) 1. Now it was Ali's chance to win the game for her team. 2. Dave liked taking his little sister Ama for walks.]

Objective: Identify details that support a main idea.

Materials: Blackline Master 16

[Answers: 1. Yes, 2. No, 3. Yes, 4. Yes, 5. No, 6. Yes, 7. Yes, 8. No]

Introduce Blackline Master 15: What's Going On?

Form student pairs of varying levels. Ask students to look at each picture and think about what is going on. Working together, have them make up a main idea sentence that gives this information. Tell them they may want to give the characters in the pictures names for this sentence. Have partners share their main idea sentences with other pairs.

Introduce Blackline Master 16: What Belongs?

Distribute copies of Blackline Master 16. Remind students that the sentences in a good paragraph all support the main idea. A sentence that does not give a supporting detail does not belong in the paragraph. Tell children to read the Main Idea sentence at the top of the page and circle either Yes or No to tell whether the sentence supports the main idea. Have partners work together to complete the activity.

Informal Assessment

Have students turn to page 35 in their textbooks. Refer them to Practice A. Have them read the Main Idea in the box and ask whether this sentence would support it: *We threw a ball around at the edge of the water.*

Assess and Reteach

Is the student able to: identify the main idea?	Reteach by allowing pre- and early production students to pantomime or draw their responses.
identify details that support the main idea?	Reteach by using the Reteach activity on TE page 35.

What's Going On?

Look at each picture. Write a sentence that gives the main idea about each picture. You can give the characters names if you wish.

What Belongs?

Read the Main Idea sentence at the top of the page. Read each sentence below. If the sentence supports the main idea, circle yes. If it does not support the main idea, circle no.

Main Idea Sentence:
Aunt June and Uncle Pete rented a boat and took us sailing.

1. The wind was just right for sailing.   Yes   No

2. Aunt June is from Iowa.   Yes   No

3. The boat moved along smoothly.   Yes   No

4. We stopped at an island for a picnic lunch.   Yes   No

5. I had eaten eggs and toast for breakfast.   Yes   No

6. When the sky turned gray, we went home.   Yes   No

7. Uncle Pete said it would be too dangerous
to sail in the storm.   Yes   No

8. I hate it when it snows in the winter, too.   Yes   No

Introduce this lesson before Pupil Edition pages 44–59.

I. PREWRITE
Oral Warm Up

Objectives:
• Ask and respond to questions
• Relate observations and recollections about an experience

TPR

Whole Group Oral Language Activity

Display assorted pictures of people and animals, and an assortment of stuffed animals and puppets. Ask: What kind of animals are these? Are the people children or adults? Have students pass the items around, giving them time to touch or look at each one. As they examine the objects, ask them to brainstorm words they would use to describe their feelings about each one. (Examples: *friendly, soft, funny, warm, pretty*). Encourage students to tell what they think each person or animal can do. (For example: *race, work, eat, cuddle, smile, sing*). Then ask: How would you describe each person or animal's personality? For example: *Does this man look happy? Is a cat playful?* Have students answer in complete sentences.

Objectives:
• Begin prewriting for a personal narrative
• Organize Ideas

Materials: Blackline Master 17; pencils

Introduce the Writing Mode

Explain that a personal narrative is a true story about their own experiences. It tells a story through the writer's own feelings and observations. Model a personal narrative about one of the pictures. *(Example: I saw a picture of a man this morning. I think he is going fishing. I went fishing last summer at the lake. I didn't catch anything all day. The night before we left I got one tiny fish! We threw it back into the lake, but I was happy anyway.)* Invite volunteers to use the chart to relate or act out a personal reaction to one of the subjects.

Pre-Production and Early Production

Graphic Organizer

Blackline Master 17

Speech Emergence

Intermediate and Advanced Fluency

Scaffolded Writing Instruction

Using Blackline Master 17, have students choose a person or animal to draw in the large circle. They can use the pictures to orally explain their ideas.

Ask students to label their pictures with words or phrases.

Have students label their drawings with sentences that begin with "I."

Research and Inquiry: Conduct an Interview

Model how to conduct an interview by asking a student about the subject they drew in Blackline Master 17. Write the questions on the board. Then have partners ask each question and record their partner's answer.

II. DRAFT

Objectives:
- Organize main ideas and details in sequence
- Begin to draft a personal narrative

TPR

Focus on Personal Narrative

Write the following sentences and then read them aloud: *My friend Billy brought me a cookie this morning. I opened the door when Billy knocked. First, he said hello. Next, he handed me a cookie he had made. Then he ran off as fast as he could go.* Point out that sentences in a personal narrative use *I, my*, or *me.* Ask: Who is my story about? (Billy) What is the main event? (Billy bringing a cookie). Write the labels *First, Next,* and *Last.* Reread the sentences and have students tell what happened in the beginning, middle, and end, then record them on the chart.

When the chart is complete, have volunteers circle the time-order words. Then ask a volunteer to circle the words *I, my,* and *me.*

Scaffolded Writing Instruction

Pre-Production & Early Production

Blackline Master 18— What Happened When?

Use Blackline Master 18 to help students draw or use a photograph to define the main idea of their personal narrative. Then have them draw the events that happened first, next, and last.

Speech Emergence

Blackline Master 19—Who? What Happened?

Using Blackline Master 19, have students use drawings as well as words and phrases to draft a personal narrative. Encourage them to write the person's name and to write time-order words such as *first, next, then, last, finally,* to explain sequence. Have them use *I, me,* and *my.*

Intermediate and Advanced Fluency

Students may begin to draft their personal narratives. Remind them that a personal narrative tells a true story about the writer's life. Encourage them to use *I, me,* and *my.* Remind them that narratives have an interesting beginning, middle, and end and that they should use time-order words. Ask students to write one or two sentences in each box.

III. REVISE

Focus on Elaboration

Write the following sentences on the board: *Next, he handed me a cookie he had made. It was almost bigger than he was!* Add this sentence to the end of the paragraph: *I think Billy is very funny.* Point out that the details about the cookies, and telling how you feel about Billy makes the story more interesting. Ask students to suggest other details from the paragraph.

Scaffolded Instruction for Revising

Have students add details to their work in Blackline Master 18. Suggest that they add additional details to their pictures.

Students can use their work in Blackline Master 19 to add details by writing words and phrases, or by drawing. Encourage them to think about how things look, sound, feel, or taste.

Have students add details that help describe how someone looks of acts, or how they felt about what happened.

Technology Link

Have partners type their drafts of their personal narratives on a computer. Then have them practice using the insert function to add detail to their stories.

IV. REVISE • PEER CONFERENCING

Objectives:
- Participate in peer conferences
- Exchange suggestions for improvement and positive comments
- Revise a personal narrative

Focus on Peer Conferencing

Partner pre-production and early production students to retell what they see in the pictures in first, next, and last order. Model questions that students may ask after reading: *Did this happen last? Does this picture tell about the main idea?* Pair intermediate and advanced fluency students and have them identify and discuss the beginning, middle, and ending of their narratives and suggest time-order words that may clarify sequence.

V. PROOFREAD

Objectives:
- Use complete sentences
- Practice proofreading strategies

Blackline Master 20

Objective: Recognize and make complete sentences.

[**Answers:** 1. Ray, Sam, Jamal, and I. When Kristen jumped on her bike. We all went to Kristen's house. (circle) Do you know the address? (circle) The house is near the.
2. Answers will vary.]

Focus on English Conventions

Say and write the following sentence fragments:

> *Went to the store.*
> *Uncle Bill bought a.*

Review that a sentence expresses a complete thought. Ask students: Who went to the store? *What did Uncle Bill buy?* Then have students complete Blackline Master 20. Model looking up the spelling of a word in a dictionary. Begin by asking students the first letter or letters of the word. Flag the word with a post-it and pass the dictionary around the class.

Have students circle words they are not sure are spelled correctly and then work with partners or small groups to help correct spelling.

VI. PUBLISH

Use page 56 as a guide for a checklist for each language proficiency level.

Dramatize a Personal Narrative

Objectives: Give an oral presentation of a personal narrative accompanied by illustrations.
TPR

Place students in mixed language-level groups. Have students practice reading their personal narratives aloud or presenting their drawings and speaking about them aloud. Encourage students who use pictures to point to specific details of pictures as they speak about them. Suggest that a volunteer display the picture for viewers so that the speaker is free to use his or her hands while talking.

VII. LISTENING, SPEAKING, VIEWING, REPRESENTING

Extension: Invite more proficient students to record the oral narratives presented by pre-production and early-production students.

Invite ESL students to present their narratives first in English, and then in their native languages. As they listen, remind them to look at the visuals as well as to listen to the words to form meanings.

Have students participate in a vocal exercise to show how inflection helps convey the meaning of words. Help them practice ways to say: *I was so surprised! You'd better hurry! I ran ahead. Did you see that?*

Informal Assessment

When assessing students' learning, you will need to adapt your expectations of what constitutes an appropriate response. For example, you may wish to have students act out or draw a response to a prompt.

Idea Web

Choose a person or animal to write about. Draw the picture of your character in the big circle. Draw or write to show what you like about the person or animal. Then draw or write something the person or animal can do.

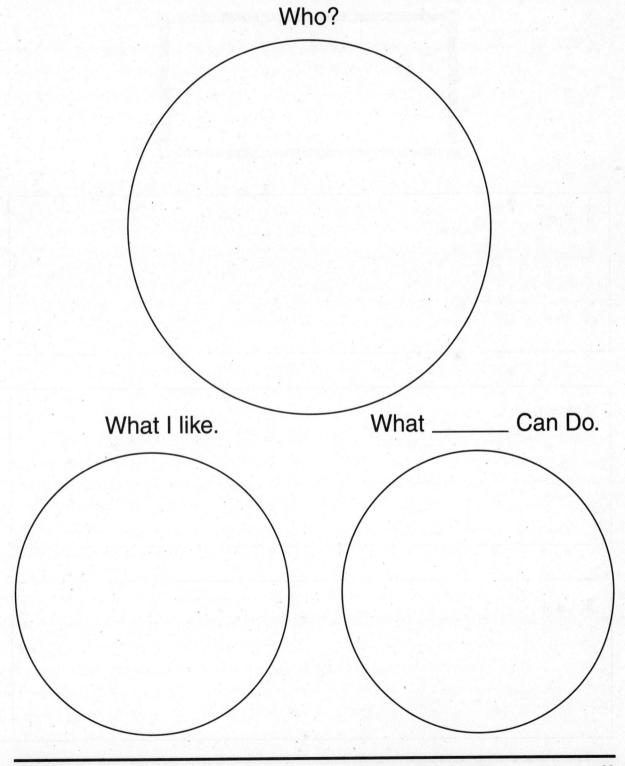

Who?

What I like.   What _____ Can Do.

Name_____ Date_____

What Happened When?

Draw the main idea of your personal narrative. Draw a picture of the event that happened first. Draw a picture of the event that happened next. Finally, draw a picture of the event that happened last.

1. First

2. Next

3. Last

Who? What Happened?

Tell about something that happened with someone you know. Write one sentence that tells the main idea of what happened. Then, fill in the boxes. Write one or two sentences that tell the events that happened first, next, and last. Then draw pictures to tell more about your story.

Personal Narrative

Main Idea

First,

Next,

Last,

Complete Sentences

A. Circle the words that make complete sentences.

Ray, Sam, Jamal and I.

When Kristen jumped on her bike.

We all went to Kristen's house.

Do you know the address?

The house is near the.

B. Add words to each group to make a complete thought.

1. _____ ran over to see us.

2. _____ never saw anyone look so happy.

3. Inside the envelope was _____.

4. We won a _____!

5. I couldn't believe _____.

C. Write a complete sentence to finish the story.

6. _____

SINGULAR AND PLURAL NOUNS

I. DEVELOP ORAL LANGUAGE
Oral Focus on Grammar Skill

Objective: Orally identify nouns and tell whether they are singular or plural.

Whole Group Oral Language Activity

Ask students to look around the classroom or outside and notice familiar objects and people, such as *desk, school, teacher.* Write these words on the chalkboard and say: *These are nouns. A noun is a word that names a person (teacher), place (school) or thing (desk). A singular noun names one person, place, or thing.* Have students repeat the definition and examples with you. Then list a few more singular nouns as examples.

Next add *s* to a few of the nouns on the chalkboard. Have students say the nouns with you. Tell students that a plural noun names more than one person, place, or thing. Then write *bird* on the chalkboard. Ask students to count the birds on page 80. When they give you a number, write it before *bird* and add *s (birds).* Say: *You add* s *to most nouns to make the plural.* Write this formula on the chalkboard: *bird + s = birds.* Have students recite this formula with you for several more plural nouns.

Scaffolded Verbal Prompting

Use the following verbal prompts to help students better understand singular and plural nouns.

Nonverbal Prompt for Active Participation

Pre-Production: *Look at the pictures. Point to one (fox). Point to the plural form of fox.*

One- or Two-Word Response Prompt

Early Production: *Say the noun. What do you add to form the plural? Say the plural form.*

Prompt for Short Answers to Higher-Level Thinking Skills

Speech Emergence: *Tell me the name of something you see displayed. Say in a sentence whether it is singular or plural. How do you make the other form?*

Prompt for Detailed Answers to Higher-Level Thinking Skills

Intermediate and Advanced Fluency: *How do you know whether a noun is singular or plural?*

II. DEVELOP GRAMMAR SKILLS IN CONTEXT
Visual/Physical Focus on Grammar Skill

Objective: Develop and demonstrate understanding of singular and plural nouns.

Blackline Master 21

TPR

Extension: Ask volunteers to draw a line under nouns in the sentences you wrote and tell whether they are singular or plural.

Extension: Have one pair of students read their piles of cards aloud to another pair of students and compare them. Challenge students to discuss and resolve any differences in their piles.

Whole Group Activity

Write a sentence on the chalkboard such as *The boy counted bugs in the jar.* Circle the nouns *boy, bugs, jar.* Provide each student with a copy of Blackline Master 21. Ask students to use crayons to color the *Singular* card green and the *Plural* card orange. Have students cut out each card. As you read the sentence aloud, invite students to hold up the green "Singular" card when they hear "boy" and "jar" and the orange "Plural" card when they hear "bugs." Invite volunteers to read the sentence aloud slowly as students hold up the correct cards. Repeat with other sentences.

Small Group Activity

Write a list of sentences with singular and plural nouns. *(Students read books in the library. My sisters like the jungle gym on the playground. Visitors saw statues in the museum.)* Give students in each group the labels of *singular* and *plural.* As you read the sentences aloud, invite students with each kind of label to jump up and say *singular* or *plural* when they hear a noun that matches their label.

Partner Activity

For each pair of students, make a set of noun cards with words such as *sister, uncles, ocean, mountains, bicycle, backpacks,* and so on. Then make two cards labeled *singular* and *plural* and place them in front of partners. Model how to sort the noun cards into the two categories and then have students sort their cards into piles.

Technology Link

Type a few sentences from a book students are familiar with into a word processing program. Pair students of different language levels. Have students underline the nouns in the sentences and type *singular* or *plural* in parentheses next to each one.

III. PRACTICE GRAMMAR SKILLS
Written Focus on Grammar Skill

Use the following Blackline masters to reinforce unit grammar skills.

Introduce Blackline Master 22: Place the Pictures

Objective: Place labeled noun pictures in sentence blanks.

Materials: Blackline Master 22

[**Answers:** mother, shells, beach; friends, path, cameras; umbrella, park, sister]

Explain to students that they will complete sentences by adding singular or plural nouns. Divide the class into pairs. Distribute Blackline Master 22. Read aloud and discuss the directions with students. Encourage students to read the completed sentences to each other.

Informal Assessment

Have students turn to page 80 in their textbooks. Read aloud a few nouns from the Guided Practice. Ask: *Is this noun singular or plural? How do you know?*

Introduce Blackline Master 23: Where Do the Nouns Belong?

Objective: Write underlined nouns in the categories *singular* and *plural*.

Materials: Blackline Master 23; pencil or pen

[**Answers:** singular: mother, father, grandfather, national park, lake, ranger, book, night, aunt, restaurant, ice cream; Plural: tents, bears, snakes, birds, sounds, insects, sandwiches]

Distribute Blackline Master 23 to pairs of students. Discuss the illustration and read the paragraph aloud. Ask students to repeat the underlined nouns after you. Read the directions aloud and together write the word *mother* in the chart under singular. Ask pairs to continue filling in the chart together.

Informal Assessment

Have students turn to page 81 in their textbooks. Point to the photo and say: *Imagine the people are on a picnic. What do you think they will see on their picnic?* As students answer, write nouns on the chalkboard. Then ask students to add these nouns to the chart on Blackline Master 23 in the correct categories.

Use the following chart to assess and reteach:

Are students able to:	
orally name singular and plural nouns?	Reteach using the Language Support Activity on TE page 80.
state the two endings of plural nouns?	Reteach using the Language Support Activity on TE page 84.
categorize nouns as singular and plural?	Reteach using the Reteach Activity on TE page 81.

Singular and Plural Noun Labels

SINGULAR

PLURAL

Name_____ Date_____

What's in the Pictures?

Underline the correct noun under each picture. Then write the words in the sentences below.

shell, shells

mother, mothers

beach, beaches

My _____ picked up _____ on the _____.

camera, cameras

friend, friends

path, paths

The _____ hiked along the _____ with their _____.

park, parks

sister, sisters

umbrella, umbrellas

The _____ in the _____ belonged to my _____.

Where Do the Nouns Belong?

Read the paragraph. Write each underlined noun in the correct column in the chart below.

My <u>mother</u> and <u>father</u>, <u>grandfather</u>, and I camped in a <u>national park</u>. We pitched our <u>tents</u> near the <u>lake</u>. A <u>ranger</u> talked about <u>bears</u> and <u>snakes</u>. We looked up new <u>birds</u> in a <u>book</u>. I liked the <u>sounds</u> of the <u>insects</u> at <u>night</u>. Then my <u>aunt</u> met us in the <u>restaurant</u>. We ate <u>sandwiches</u> and <u>ice cream</u>.

Singular	Plural

I. DEVELOP ORAL LANGUAGE
Oral Focus on Grammar Skill

Objective: Orally describe pictures and identify plural nouns with –ies and irregular plural nouns.

Whole Group Oral Language Activity

Ask students to look at the photograph on page 82. Ask: *What are the man and the boy looking at?* (butterflies) *What would you call just one of them?* (butterfly) Write students' response on the chalkboard. Say: *To form the plural of nouns ending in a consonant and y, change the y to i and add –es.* Ask a volunteer to help you change *butterfly* to *butterflies.* Then write the formula: *butterfly → butterfli + es → butterflies.* Have students say both the singular and plural forms with you.

Remind students that a noun is a word that names something—a person, place, or thing—and that a singular noun names one and a plural noun names more than one. Show students one penny. Ask them to say the singular and plural forms with you. Then use the format on page 82 to demonstrate again how to form the plural *(penny → penni + es = pennies).* Invite students to recite the formula with you. Now display pictures of bunnies and daisies and write the words under them. Repeat the formulas for the plural.

Next introduce irregular plurals. Explain that some nouns have special plural forms. Write tooth on the chalkboard. Ask: *Do you know what the plural of* tooth *is?* Write <u>teeth</u> and underline the changed letters. Highlight a few more examples from the chart on page 84, prompting students to recite the singular and plural forms with you.

Scaffolded Verbal Prompting

Use the following verbal prompts to help students better understand plural nouns with –ies.

Nonverbal Prompt for Active Participation

Pre-Production: *Look at the photograph. Point to one butterfly. Now point to more than one butterfly. Show me the plural form of butterfly.*

One- or Two-Word Response Prompt

Early Production: *Say the name of a noun whose picture you see. What three letters form the plural? Say the plural form.*

Prompt for Short Answers to Higher-Level Thinking Skills

Speech Emergence: *Tell me the name of a picture you see displayed. Say in a sentence whether it is singular or plural. Tell me how you make the plural form with –ies.*

Prompt for Detailed Answers to Higher-Level Thinking Skills

Intermediate and Advanced Fluency: *How do you form the plural of nouns ending in* y?

II. DEVELOP GRAMMAR SKILLS IN CONTEXT
Visual/Physical Focus on Grammar Skill

Objective: Develop and demonstrate understanding of plural nouns with –*ies*.

Blackline Master 24

TPR

Extension: Ask students to take turns at the chalkboard changing singular forms of nouns ending in consonant and *y* to plural forms. Provide the format on page 82 for students to fill in.

Extension: Challenge one partner to read a noun card aloud and the other partner to spell the word aloud without looking at the card. Then have partners switch roles.

Whole Group Activity

Write sentences on the chalkboard with some of the words in the Guided Practice on page 82 and include both the singular and plural forms. (Examples: *I read three of the story/stories in this book. My grandmother owns a bakery/bakeries. Two family/families live in the house next door.*) Provide each student with a copy of Blackline Master 24. Invite them to draw a decorative border around each card and cut out the cards. As you read each sentence, say both versions of the noun. Then ask students to hold up either the *y* or the *ies* card, and say the correct form. Circle the correct form of the noun and have students read the sentence aloud with you. Repeat with more sentences.

Small Group Activity

Write a list of words ending in a consonant and *y;* for example *fly, city, country, grocery, spy, secretary.* As you say each word and its plural, ask either one or more students to stand up in each group and hold up either their *y* or *ies* cards.

Partner Activity

Assign one partner the *y* card and one student the *ies* card. Provide a list of singular and plural nouns from this lesson written on separate cards. Have partners read the noun cards and each take the ones belonging to his or her ending. Then have partners switch noun cards and write the other form (singular or plural) on the back.

Technology Link

Provide a list of singular and plural nouns from this lesson in a word processing program. Ask partners of different language levels to work together to change the singular nouns to plural and the plural nouns to singular.

III. PRACTICE GRAMMAR SKILLS
Written Focus on Grammar Skill

Use the following blackline masters to reinforce unit grammar skills.

Introduce Blackline Master 25: How Many?

Objective: Draw the correct number of objects and write the plural form of the noun.

Materials: Blackline Master 25; crayons or colored pencils

[Answers: (six) daisies; (five) candies; (7) cherries; (3) jellies]

Reinforce that plural means more than one by placing first one penny on your desk and then several. Ask a volunteer to count the pennies. Write *penny/pennies* on the chalkboard. Distribute Blackline Master 25. Read aloud and discuss the directions with students. Have students complete the page, then exchange with a partner to check the correct spelling of each plural. Ask volunteers to write the plural forms on the chalkboard.

Informal Assessment

Refer students to page 82 of their textbooks. Read aloud some nouns from the Guided Practice and ask: *What is the plural form? Can you write it on the chalkboard?*

Introduce Blackline Master 26: Count and Write Plurals

Objective: Count the number of items in the picture and write that number and the plural of the noun.

Materials: Blackline Master 26; pen or pencil

[Answers: 1. three countries 2. ten cherries 3. Two families 4. four bunnies 5. Eight strawberries]

Show or draw a picture of four daisies. Write this sentence frame on the chalkboard: *We picked _____ _____.* Ask a volunteer to count the daisies. Then ask: *How many daisies are there? How do we change the word* daisy *to make it plural?* Write the student's response on the blanks in the sentence. Then read the completed sentence. Distribute Blackline Master 26. Read aloud and discuss the directions with students. Ask pairs to complete the exercise together.

Informal Assessment

Turn to page 82 of the textbook. Point to the photo and say: *This boy builds model planes for a hobby. How do you write the singular and plural forms of* hobby? *of* lily? story? lady?

Use the following chart to assess and reteach:

Are students able to:	
orally say the plural form of nouns ending in consonant and *y?*	Reteach using the Language Support Activity on TE page 82.
change the singular forms of nouns ending in consonant and *y* to plural?	Reteach using the Reteach workbook page 17.
complete sentences with the correct plural form of nouns ending in consonant and *y?*	Reteach using the Reteach Activity on TE page 83.

Plural Noun Endings

y

ies

How many?

Read the noun below each picture frame. Draw as many of each noun as there are spaces. Write the plural form of the noun on the line.

daisy _____

candy _____

cherry _____

jelly _____

Count and Write Plurals

Read the sentences and look at the pictures. In the first blank, write how many. In the second blank write the plural of the noun next to the picture.

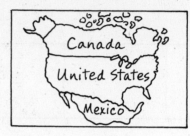

country

1. The map shows _____ _____.

cherry

2. There are _____ _____ on the cake.

family

3. _____ _____ are taking pictures.

bunny

4. My brother has _____ _____ in one cage.

strawberry

5. Marie picked _____ _____ for her breakfast.

I. DEVELOP ORAL LANGUAGE
Oral Focus on Grammar Skill

Objective: Orally explain the difference between proper and common nouns.

Whole Group Oral Language Activity

Write the word *river* on the chalkboard and ask: *Is this a common noun or a proper noun?* Explain that common nouns name any person, place, or thing, but that proper nouns name special things and begin with a capital letter. Write *Nile River* on the chalkboard and say: *This is a proper noun because it names a special river and begins with capital letters.* Have students repeat the common and proper nouns after you.

Remind students that a noun is a word that names something—a person, place, or thing. Point to the picture of a bus on page 87, the jar on page 82, and the airplane on page 83. Write these nouns on the chalkboard. Say: *Repeat these common nouns after me.* Then write and have students say a few more examples of common nouns.

Show pictures of places, such as the Washington Monument, the Great Pyramids, the Grand Canyon. Choose a student to point to each picture as you say what it is. Then write the names next to the pictures. Ask: *Which letters are capitals? Underline the letters. What do they tell you about the noun?* Then write the common noun next to each name; for example, *monument, pyramid, canyon.* Have students say all the nouns with you and identify them as common or proper (Great Pyramids, proper; canyon, common). Repeat with other examples of proper nouns and their common nouns.

Scaffolded Verbal Prompting

Use the following verbal prompts to help students better understand common and proper nouns.

Nonverbal Prompt for Active Participation

Pre-Production: *Look at the pictures I point to. Clap your hands if the word is a proper noun.*

One- or Two-Word Response Prompt

Early Production: *Say the name of something in one of the pictures. Tell me the common noun that goes with that picture.*

Prompt for Short Answers to Higher-Level Thinking Skills

Speech Emergence: *Tell me a special word that names a (river). How do you know if that is a common or a proper noun?*

Prompt for Detailed Answers to Higher-Level Thinking Skills

Intermediate and Advanced Fluency: *Name a pair of nouns, one common and one proper, that refer to the same thing. Tell me the special way you write the proper noun.*

II. DEVELOP GRAMMAR SKILLS IN CONTEXT
Visual/Physical Focus on Grammar Skill

Objective: Develop and demonstrate understanding of common and proper nouns.

Blackline Master 27

[**Answers:** Lake Ontario, Oregon, Mr. Osgood, Atex Foods, Cincinnati, April, Maple Street, Yellowstone Park, Alexis, Pike's Peak]

TPR

Extension: Invite students to take turns saying a noun from the list while the other students turn the list over. Volunteers then say whether the noun is proper or common. They then look at the list to check their answers.

Extension: Have pairs of students write or say sentences using common and proper nouns from Blackline Master 27. Write some of the sentences on the chalkboard and have volunteers underline the common nouns and circle the proper nouns.

Whole Group Activity

Write on the chalkboard pairs of common nouns and proper nouns without capitals, such as *australia/continent* and *zoo/national zoo*. Replace the first letter of each word with a write-on line. Ask: *Which words are proper nouns? Where do the capital letters belong?* Invite volunteers to write the appropriate lowercase or capital letter on each line.

Distribute copies of Blackline Master 27 to students. Read all the nouns aloud and invite students to say them after you. Then instruct them to cut out the capital letters and glue them on the correct lines below the proper nouns. Write each proper noun, with capitals, on the chalkboard. Suggest that students draw small illustrations for any words they want.

Small Group Activity

Give each group a list of common and proper nouns in random order. Appoint a group leader who holds two cards with *common* and *proper* written on them. The leader holds up one card and the rest of the group claps when they see a noun of that kind in the list. The leader calls on the first student who clapped to stand and say the noun. Check that noun off the list and continue until all the nouns are chosen.

Partner Activity

Give each pair of students several cards with common nouns written on them and the same number of cards with matching proper nouns (for example, *city, Philadelphia; river, Mississippi River; school, Pioneer Elementary*). Have students turn the cards down, mix them up, and play a matching game. Students take turns turning over two cards at a time to look for matching pairs.

Technology Link

Ask students to go to a web page that you choose for them. Tell them to write all the proper nouns they find, then type the proper nouns into a word processing program. Students can begin an electronic class book of proper nouns.

III. PRACTICE GRAMMAR SKILLS
Written Focus on Grammar Skill

Use the following Blackline masters to reinforce unit grammar skills.

Introduce Blackline Master 28: Common Nouns and Proper Nouns

Objective: Classify common and proper nouns.

Materials: Blackline Master 28; pen or pencil

Write *team* and *New York Yankees* on the chalkboard. Ask: *What is the same about these two things?* (The Yankees are an example of a team.) Invite students to help you create a sentence using both words, such as *The New York Yankees are my uncle's favorite baseball team.* Distribute Blackline Master 28. Read aloud and discuss the directions with students. Then have students complete the page in pairs.

Informal Assessment

Write the list headings *Common* and *Proper* on the chalkboard. Call out several common and proper nouns and have students tell you where to write them.

Introduce Blackline Master 29: Common and Proper Nouns

Objective: Write the correct common or proper noun.

Materials: Blackline Master 29; pen or pencil

Explain that proper nouns can be specific examples of common nouns, for example, Idaho (proper noun) is an example of a state (common noun). Distribute Blackline Master 29. Read aloud and discuss the directions with students. Tell them to read the words and look at the pictures in the boxes for clues about which word in the list matches. When students have completed the page, have partners exchange their work and check for correctness.

Informal Assessment

Read sentences from More Practice on page 87. Ask: *Is (Sam Griffin, neighbors) a common or proper noun?*

Use the following chart to assess and reteach.

Are students able to:	
orally name common and proper nouns?	Reteach using the Language Support Activity on TE page 86.
correct proper nouns for capitalization?	Reteach using the Rules Box on PE page 86.
list nouns in *common* and *proper* categories?	Reteach using the Reteach Activity on TE page 87.

Replace the Letters

| C | S | A | M | P | Y | P | A | P | O | L | O | F | A | O | M |

lake lake ontario ___ ___ ___	oregon state ___ ___
teacher mr. osgood ___ ___ ___	company atex foods ___ ___ ___
cincinnati city ___ ___	april month ___ ___
street maple street ___ ___ ___	yellowstone park park ___ ___ ___
alexis girl ___ ___	mountain pike's peak ___ ___ ___

Common Nouns and Proper Nouns

Cut out the words. Paste them on the correct computer
screen. Then draw lines to connect the common nouns
with their proper noun examples.

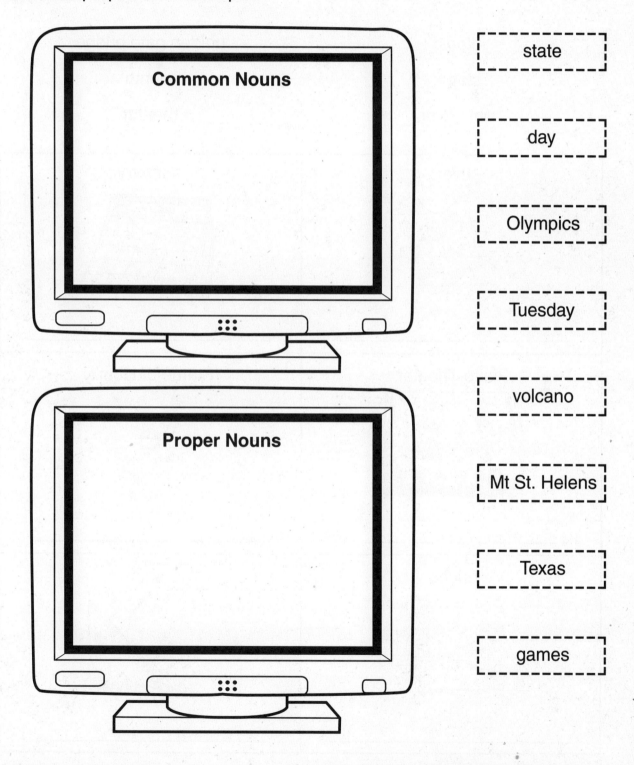

state

day

Olympics

Tuesday

volcano

Mt St. Helens

Texas

games

Common and Proper Nouns

Read the words in the boxes and look at the pictures. Choose a word from the list that completes the labels in the boxes. Write the word on the line, using capital letters when necessary.

titanic	golden gate bridge
statue	month
ohio river	theater

river 	January 
_____	_____

Rialto Theater 	Statue of Liberty 
_____	_____

bridge 	ship 
_____	_____

SINGULAR AND PLURAL POSSESSIVE NOUNS

I. DEVELOP ORAL LANGUAGE
Oral Focus on Grammar Skill

Objective: Orally identify *apostrophe s* as the singular possessive form

Whole Group Oral Language Activity

Discuss the illustrations on pages 90 and 91. Write these two phrases on the chalkboard: *The boy has a horse. The man has a hat.* Then write these sentences below the first two: *The horse is big. The hat is small.* Then demonstrate how you can express each thought in a single sentence using the possessive form: *The boy's horse is big. The man's hat is small.* Discuss the punctuation we use to show possession: apostrophe. Demonstrate the plural possessive the same way with the illustrations on pages 92 (lions' rock) and 93 (boys' notes), allowing students to say the correct possessive forms.

Scaffolded Verbal Prompting

Use the following verbal prompts to help students better understand singular and plural possessive nouns.

Nonverbal Prompt for Active Participation

Pre-Production: *Point to (lion cub and mother lion). If I say* the lions' rock, *show me where the apostrophe goes.*

One- or Two-Word Response Prompt

Early Production: *How many (boys) are in this picture (p. 90)? How many boys are in this picture (p. 93)? Say and point to the singular possessive noun on the chalkboard. Now say and point to the plural possessive noun.*

Prompt for Short Answers to Higher-Level Thinking Skills

Speech Emergence: *Tell me how many (lions) are in this picture. How do you know that (lions') is plural possessive?*

Prompt for Detailed Answers to Higher-Level Thinking Skills

Intermediate and Advanced Fluency: *Finish these sentences: To make* boy *singular possessive, add _____ (an apostrophe and an s). To make* lions *plural possessive, add _____ (an apostrophe).*

II. DEVELOP GRAMMAR SKILLS IN CONTEXT
Visual/Physical Focus on Grammar Skill

Objective: Develop and demonstrate understanding of singular and plural possessive nouns.

Blackline Master 30

TPR

Extension: Ask partners to write the singular or plural possessives of the nouns they found in the paragraph. Collect all the lists into a class book of singular and plural possessives.

Whole Group Activity

Write two sentences on the chalkboard such as *My sister has an iguana. The students have a turtle.* Ask students to go to the chalkboard and circle the nouns to be made possessive. Then point to the word *sister* and say: *We can make this noun possessive in the phrase:* My sister's iguana. *What do we add to* sister *to make it possessive?* Invite students to hum and hold up the correct card ('s). Write the phrase on the chalkboard. Repeat with the other sentence, teaching the ' ending. Finally, write: *The children have a bird.* Teach that we add *'s* to plural nouns that do not end in *s.*

Provide each student with a copy of Blackline Master 30. Instruct students to draw a decorative border around each card and cut out the cards.

Small Group Activity

Give each group a list of singular and plural nouns, including some plurals that do not end in *s.* Place the three cards from Blackline Master 30 on a desk. Ask students to cut apart the list of nouns and place them in appropriate piles under each card, according to how they form the possessive. Then have groups switch desks and check each other's piles.

Partner Activity

Copy a paragraph from a book onto large paper. Give a different paragraph to each pair of students. Ask partners to cut out all the singular and plural nouns and put them in piles under the three cards from Blackline Master 30, according to how they form the possessive.

Technology Link

Have students type their lists of singular and plural possessive nouns into a word processing program. Encourage students to add to the list when they discover new nouns.

III. PRACTICE GRAMMAR SKILLS
Written Focus on Grammar Skill

Use the following Blackline masters to reinforce unit grammar skills.

Introduce Blackline Master 31: Put It Together

Objective: identify the correct possessive ending and write the possessive noun.

Materials: Blackline Master 31; pen or pencil

[**Answers:** caterpillars', penguins', geese's, alligator's, children's, cage's]

Draw three rabbits on the chalkboard. Write *rabbit + ('s, s')*. Ask a volunteer to look at the illustration and circle the correct possessive ending in parentheses. Write *rabbits'* on the chalkboard. Distribute Blackline Master 31 to students. Read the directions aloud. Tell students to complete the page. Put them in small groups to check their work. Then challenge individuals to say or write sentences using the possessive nouns.

Informal Assessment

Read aloud a noun from the Guided Practice on page 94. Ask: *Is this noun singular or plural possessive?* Challenge students to change the noun to the other number and form the possessive.

Introduce Blackline Master 32: Draw the Right Number

Objective: Make the noun either singular or plural possessive and draw one or more than one object.

Materials: Blackline Master 32; crayons or colored pencils

[**Answers:** monkey's (one); neighbor's (one); kangaroo's (one); men's (more than one); lizards' (more than one); horses' (more than one)]

Write a few singular and plural possessive nouns on the chalkboard, such as *bicycle's, hamsters'*. After each one, ask students to hold up one finger for singular and more than one finger for plural nouns. Distribute Blackline Master 32. Read aloud and discuss the directions with students. Have them complete the page on their own and compare their possessive forms and drawings with a partner's.

Informal Assessment

Read aloud sentences from More Practice on page 95. Ask volunteers to write the correct possessive form of the noun on the chalkboard. Help students with spelling as needed.

Use the following chart to assess and reteach:

Are students able to:	
orally identify singular and plural possessive nouns?	Reteach using the Language Support Activity on TE page 92.
describe the endings for singular and plural possessive nouns?	Reteach using the Language Support Activity on TE page 94.
write the singular and plural possessive forms of nouns?	Reteach using the Reteach Activity on TE pages 93 and 95.

Apostrophe Cards

's

,

's

(plural nouns that do not end in *s*)

Name _____ Date _____

Put It Together

Read the noun in the first column and look at the picture. Circle the correct ending in parentheses. Write the possessive form of the noun on the line.

caterpillar + ('s, s')		_____
penguins + (', s')		_____
geese + (', s')		_____
alligator + ('s, s')		_____
children + (', 's)		_____
cage + ('s, s')		_____

Draw the Right Number

Read the nouns. Decide the correct possessive form. Draw either one thing or more than one thing the noun names.

the monkey_____ banana	the neighbor_____ house
the kangaroo_____ baby	men_____ shirts
the lizards_____ log	the horses_____ hay

COMPOUND WORDS

Introduce this lesson before Pupil Edition pages 112–113.

I. DEVELOP ORAL LANGUAGE
Oral Focus on Vocabulary Skill

Objective: Identify and generate compound words.

Whole Group Oral Language Activity

Display a paintbrush. Ask a volunteer to name the object. Explain to students that the word *paintbrush* is made up of two smaller words. Ask students to name the two small words that they know that make up the word *paintbrush.* (paint; brush) Tell students that compound words, such as *paintbrush,* are made up of two or more smaller words. Name other compound words, such as *afternoon, seashell, birdseed, backyard,* and *outdoors.* Have volunteers name the two smaller words that make up each compound word.

Scaffolded Verbal Prompting

Use the following verbal prompts to help students better understand compound words and their meanings.

Nonverbal Prompt for Active Participation

TPR

Pre-Production: Say: *Raise your hand each time you hear me say a compound word. Put your hand down if the word is not a compound word. Ready? Listen: cupcake, sailboat, house, pancakes, computer, birthday, sweatshirt, butterfly, birdseed.*

One- or two-Word Response prompt

Early Production: *Name the two words that make up the compound word rainstorm. (rain, storm) Repeat for other words.*

Prompt for Short Answers to Higher-Level Thinking Skills

Speech Emergence: *Which of these breakfast foods is not a compound word:* pancakes, oatmeal, cereal. *Tell how you decided.*

Prompt for Detailed Answers to Higher-Level Thinking Skills

Intermediate and Advanced Fluency: *How would you explain to a student in the second grade what a compound word is? Give an example to show what you mean.*

II. DEVELOP VOCABULARY SKILLS IN CONTEXT
Visual/Physical Focus on Vocabulary Skill

Objective: Identify compound words

TPR

Small Group Activity

Write on separate index cards words that form compound words when joined. Make enough cards so that each group member gets a card. Include words that can be combined in several different ways, such as *in, out, side, doors, snow, ball, basket, man,* and *mail.* Give one card to each student. Tell students to combine their words with other words in their group to make as many compound words as they can. Then have groups act out words from their list. The rest of the class can guess the word.

Partner Activity

Have students of varying language levels work as partners. Tell partners to create at least two riddles for others to solve. They should write a compound word on a piece of drawing paper. On the flip side, they draw an addition expression that show two objects being added together. For example, for the word *toothbrush,* they would show pictures of a tooth + a brush. Have students share their riddles by showing the drawing and having other guess the compound word.

III. PRACTICE VOCABULARY SKILLS
Written Focus on Vocabulary Skill

Practice A

Blackline Master 33: Make Compound Words

Objective: Identify compound words

Materials: Blackline Master 33; pencils

[**Answers:** 1. paintbrush; 2. sailboat; 3. seashore; 4. doghouse; 5. snowman; 6. butterfly; 7. popcorn; 8. horseshoe; 9. basketball]

Practice B

Objective: Identify compound words and associate compound words with their meaning

Materials: Blackline Master 34; pencils

[**Answers:** 1. grandmother; 2. bluebird; 3. seashore; 4. starfish; 5. rowboat]

Introduce Blackline Master 33: Make Compound Words

Distribute Blackline Master 33. Review what compound words are and how they change the meaning of the individual words when put together. Read aloud the directions with students. Complete the first exercise together. Ask a volunteer to read the two words below the first picture. Discuss the meaning of each word. Have a volunteer name the item in the picture. (a paintbrush) Tell students to draw a circle around the compound word that names the picture. Check students' work. Have students complete the rest of the exercises.

Introduce Blackline Master 34: Make Compound Words

Distribute Blackline Master 34. Review what compound words are and how putting the words together changes the meaning. Read the directions with students and work through exercise 1 with them. Then ask volunteers to read the words in the box. Read exercise 1 aloud. Direct students' attention to the picture. Ask them who the girl is with in the car. (grandmother) Remind students that the word has to be a compound word. Have students look in the box to see if they can find the two words that make up the compound word for their answer. (grand, mother) Have them write the compound word on the line. Check students' work. Tell students to complete the rest of the exercises independently.

Informal Assessment

Have students turn to page 113 in the textbook. Refer them to exercise one in Practice A. Ask, *Which two words make up the compound word in the sentence?* Next, read aloud exercise 6 in Practice B. Ask, *How do you know that* outdoors *is a compound word?*

Use the following chart to assess and reteach.

Are students able to: identify compound words?	Reteach by using the Language Support Activity on TE page 112.
make compound words by putting two words together?	Reteach by using the Reteach Activity on TE page 113.

Name _____ Date _____

Find Compound Words

Look at each picture. Read the words below each picture. Circle the compound word that names each picture.

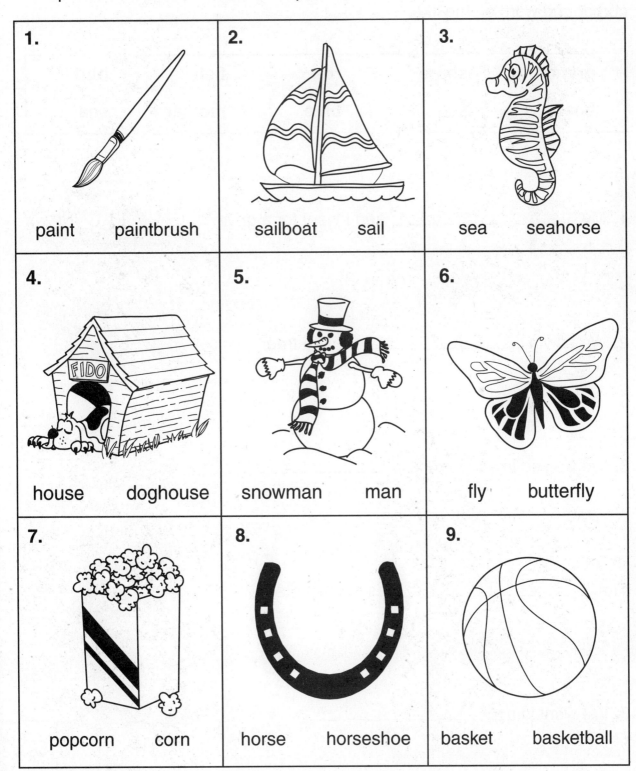

1. paint   paintbrush

2. sailboat   sail

3. sea   seahorse

4. house   doghouse

5. snowman   man

6. fly   butterfly

7. popcorn   corn

8. horse   horseshoe

9. basket   basketball

Make Compound Words

Read each sentence. Read the words in the box. Choose two words from the box to make a compound word to complete each sentence. Write the compound word on the line.

grand	**shore**	**row**	**fish**	**bird**
boat	**star**	**blue**	**mother**	**sea**

1. My _____ and I went for a drive.

2. We saw a _____ in a tree.

3. We walked in sand at the _____.

4. A _____ was in the water.

5. We went in a _____.

ORGANIZATION

BUILD SKILLS/Composition

Introduce this lesson before Pupil Edition pages 114–115.

I. DEVELOP ORAL LANGUAGE
Oral Focus on Composition Skill

Objective: Orally describe the order in which events take place.

TPR

Extension: Make a series of instructions for simple processes. Put each step on a sentence strip. Shuffle the strips, then have students put them in order. Use clue words to help them.

Nonverbal Prompt for Active Participation

One- or Two-Word Response Prompt

Prompt for Short Answers to Higher-Level Thinking Skills

Prompt for Detailed Answers to Higher-Level Thinking Skills

Whole Group Oral Language Activity

Have students look at the photograph on page 115. Discuss what the girl is holding. Ask: *Do you think the girl made the "ocean in a bottle"? How?* Lead students to see that if the girl were to explain how she made her "ocean," she would have to tell the steps in order. Say that she would use words like *first, next, then,* and *last* to show the order in which she did the steps to make the item. Have students look at Practice B on page 115. Ask them to pantomime the steps in order, while telling what they are doing in each step.

Scaffolded Verbal Prompting

Use the following verbal prompts to help students understand the importance of organization.

Pre-Production: *Show me the steps you would take to (make a sandwich, turn on the computer, and so on).*

Early Production: *Use the words* first, next, *and* last *as you act out the steps to (make a sandwich, turn on the computer, and so on).*

Speech Emergence: *Use the words* first, next, *and* last *to tell me how you do something.*

Intermediate Fluency: *Look at the picture on page 35 of your textbook. Tell me what the girl did when she got to the beach. Use the words* first, next, then, *and* last *in your sentences.*

Grade 3

Unit 2 • BUILD SKILLS/Composition **81**

II. DEVELOP COMPOSITION SKILLS IN CONTEXT
Visual/Physical Focus on Composition Skill

Objective: Play a game to determine order.

TPR

Small Group Activity

Play a *First, Next, Last* game with students. Write a series of topics on the chalkboard, such as a trip to the beach, or a walk to Grandma's. Break students into groups of three. Rotate students being the first, next, and last person to tell about a topic. For example, the first student might say: *First, I walked down my steps.* The second student might say, *Then I ran up Elm Street.* The third student might say, *Last, I came to Grandma's apartment.*

Partner Activity

Ask each partner to draw a three- or four-panel comic strip that tells what happened first, next, and last. Have them cut it into panels, mix them up, and challenge their partner to sort them into the right order.

III. PRACTICE COMPOSITION SKILLS
Written Focus on Composition Skill

Practice A

Objective: Put a series of events in order.

Materials: Blackline Master 35; scissors; crayons

[**Answers:** Panels should be rearranged in this order: bottom right, top right, bottom left, top left.]

Practice B

Objective: Put events of a story in order

Materials: Blackline Master 36; pencil

[**Answers:** first story: 3, 2, 1, 4; second story: 4, 1, 3, 2]

Introduce Blackline Master 35: Making Toast

Distribute Blackline Master 35. Go over the directions orally with students. Tell them to color each picture. As they do, they should think about an order of events that makes sense. What would come first? next? next? last? After students have completed the activity, have them discuss why they put each step where they did.

Introduce Blackline Master 36: A Mixed-Up Mess

Distribute copies of Blackline Master 36 to each student. Read the directions aloud with them. Have students work with partners of different levels to figure out the order of the sentences in each story. When they are finished, have them compare their choices with other pairs before you go over the correct answers.

Informal Assessment

Ask students to add a time-order word to these sentences to make them clearer: *We finished our game. We went home.*

Use the following chart to assess and reteach:

Are students able to: put a series of steps in order?	Reteach by allowing pre- and early production students to pantomime or draw their responses.
put story events in order?	Reteach by using Reteach Activity on TE page 115.

Making Toast

Color the pictures. Cut them out. Put them in order.

A Mixed-Up Mess

Read each group of sentences. Think about which one would happen first, next, then last. Write the number 1, 2, 3, or 4 in front of each sentence to tell the order.

_____ He yelled, "Is anybody home?"

_____ He walked into the kitchen.

_____ Tim opened the door.

_____ Grandma said, "I am! Hi, Tim!"

_____ Lana finished her homework.

_____ Lana sat down to work.

_____ Then she worked for a half hour.

_____ She took out her math book and a pencil.

Introduce this lesson before Pupil Edition pages 124–139.

I. PREWRITE
Oral Warm Up

Objectives:
• Give and respond to directions.
• Recognize steps in a process

TPR

Graphic Organizer Blackline Master 37– Sequence Chart

Objectives: Use a graphic organizer to explain steps in a process. Practice writing an explanation.

Materials: Blackline Master 37; pencils

Pre-Production and Early Production

Speech Emergence

Intermediate and Advanced Fluency

Whole Group Oral Language Activity

Tell students to follow your directions for an exercise: Stand up. Then put your arms above your head. Now put your arms down at your side. Have students sit down and ask them which words helped them follow directions (up, above, down).

Introduce the Writing Mode

Discuss that when students write directions or explain how to do something they are sharing information with other people. Remind them that you gave directions for how to do an exercise. Model explanatory writing about making spaghetti. (Example: *First, boil a pot of water. Then cook the spaghetti for 8 to 10 minutes. When it is cooked, take out the spaghetti and drain it. Finally, put a little tomato sauce on the spaghetti.*)

Scaffolded Writing Instruction

Using Blackline Master 37, have students number each box to show four steps that can be followed to make spaghetti. They can use the pictures to act out their directions.

Have students label each picture with words or phrases. Have them make additional drawings between the boxes to show any extra steps.

Have students create sentences in the boxes to give directions for making spaghetti, in the correct order.

Research and Inquiry: Use Parts of a Book

Explain that there are two parts in books that give information about what can be found in the book. The table of contents at the front of the book lists the subjects, or chapters, and page numbers of the book. At the back of the book, an index lists the titles of the subjects in alphabetical order. Point out that students can use research books to help them write an explanation of how to do something.

Model using a table of contents and an index in a class resource book. Then ask, *What word would I look up in the index of a cookbook to learn more about making spaghetti?*

II. DRAFT

Objectives:
- Use sequence strategies to organize ideas.
- Begin drafting instructions

Focus on Explanatory Writing

Model and write a topic sentence that introduces instructions for making spaghetti. *It is easy to make a good spaghetti dinner.* Ask: *What will the reader expect to find out about?* Explain that the main idea of your instructions is how to make spaghetti. Have students use their experience to help them brainstorm ideas for writing instructions and list them on the board. Then ask volunteers to use the list to give sentences or act out ideas that could introduce the subjects.

Scaffolded Writing Instruction

Pre-Production & Early Production

Blackline Master 38–Step 1, Step 2, Step 3, Step 4

Use Blackline Master 38 to help students organize in sequence their explanations of how to do something. Have them draw or cut-out pictures, and encourage them to show the materials that are needed in each step.

Speech Emergence

Blackline Master 39–What To Do, What You Need, How To Do It

Use Blackline Master 39 to guide students in their explanatory writing. Have them draw and write words or short phrases for their instructions. Encourage them to use time-order words as they explain their instructions.

Intermediate and Advanced Fluency

Students may begin writing their instructions. Encourage students to begin by writing a topic sentence that introduces the main idea and that will make readers interested in following their instructions. Then have them add details about the materials that will be needed. Remind students to give the instructions for the activity in step-by-step order. Invite them to illustrate their topic in the top box.

III. REVISE

Objectives:
- Revise explanatory writing.
- Add details with time-order and spatial words

Focus on Elaboration

Have students use a book or a paper cup and give the following commands: *Look inside your book. Put your hand beside your book. Hold your hand above your book. Hold your hand below your book. Point to the top of the book. Show me the outside of the book. Show me the inside.* Then help students visualize location by drawing some squares on the board. Then draw Xs to indicate a location and ask students, for example: *Is this inside or outside?* Write the spatial word above the diagram.

TPR

Explain that words like *bottom, below,* and *over* explain where things are in space or where things go, and that using these words will help them write clear instructions.

Pre-Production & Early
Production
Blackline Master 38–Step 1,
Step 2, Step 3, Step 4
Speech Emergence
Blackline Master 39–What To
Do, What You Need, How to
Do It
Intermediate and Advanced
Fluency

Scaffolded Instruction for Revising

Have students add details to their work in Blackline Master 38 by adding or changing their drawings to show location.

Use student's work on Blackline Master 39 to help them elaborate by adding details that explain location and time-order. Have them add words, short phrases, or pictures that give more information.

Students may elaborate by giving details about location and time-order, and by writing additional phrases or sentences that explain words that are specific to their instructions; for example, *boil, beat* (an egg), *glue.*

Technology Link

Have partners use the thesaurus in the Tools menu to look for words that describe location. For example, by typing the word *above,* the thesaurus will list words and phrases like *on top of.*

IV. REVISE: Peer Conferencing

Focus on Peer Conferencing

Objectives:
• Participate in peer conferences.
• Give and receive suggestions for improvement.
• Revise explanatory writing.

Pair more fluent speakers with pre-production and early production students who will retell their explanations from their drawings. Encourage more fluent speakers to supply English vocabulary words as they retell their partners' stories.

Use page 133 as a guide and write a checklist for each language proficiency level on the chalkboard. Readers can refer to them as they hold their peer conferences.

V. PROOFREAD

Focus on English Conventions

Objectives:
• Use complete sentences.
• Practice proofreading strategies.
• Use singular and plural nouns.

Materials: Blackline Master 40; pencils

[**Answers:** A. 1. jar, 2. houses, 3. dishes, 4. birds, 5. pencils; B. 6. kites, 7. brushes, 8. bottles, 9. pieces, 10. boxes]

Spelling Tip: List these rules on the board: Nouns that end in *s, x, c, z,* and *sh* form a plural by adding *-es.* Nouns that end in a vowel and *y* add *-s.* Nouns that end with a consonant and *y* change *y* to *i* and add *-es.*

Say and write the following sentences: *You need two egg. Put glue on one sticks. Fill a glasses to the top.* Point out that most plural nouns end in *-s* or *-es.* Ask volunteers what is wrong with each sentence and re-write the nouns correctly. *(eggs, stick, glass.)*

Have students complete Blackline Master 40 to practice the grammar skill. Explain that when students proofread their work, they look for mistakes and correct them. Ask students to reread their sentences to make sure that they have used singular and plural nouns correctly.

Explain that proofreading includes checking for spelling mistakes. When students ask for help in spelling a word, help them sound it out as you write the word in a Word Box on the board. When other students ask for help with a word, have them check the Word Box to see if that word is there.

VI. PUBLISH

Objective: Give an oral presentation of a personal narrative accompanied by illustrations.

Use page 136 as a guide and write and read aloud a checklist for each proficiency level. Encourage students to use the checklist as they prepare final drafts.

TPR

Create a Book of Projects

Place small groups of students in mixed language-level groups. Before assembling their books, have students share their explanatory pieces by talking about their pictures or reading their explanatory writing. Encourage each student to ask the author a question about their experiences with their subject, such as: *About how long does it take to do this? How did you learn to do this? Do you do this every day?*

Extension: If time allows and materials are available, help the class choose one explanatory paragraph and follow the instructions to complete a project.

Students who drew pictures may choose to ask others to help them write titles or add words to their work. Write the following guidelines for making a book and read them aloud:

• Add drawings to your writing or take photographs of a finished project.

• Make a table of contents for your book, using the title of each student's work.

• Put the group's writing in a folder, following the order of the table of contents.

• Write a title for your book and display it in the classroom.

VII. LISTENING, SPEAKING, VIEWING, REPRESENTING

TPR

Invite ESL students to present their instructions first in their native languages and then to act out their instructions as they give them in English. Have students who speak the same language comment on their work first in their native language, and then in English. As students listen, remind them to look at the visuals as well as to listen to the words to form meaning. Remind fluent speakers to use gestures that will help convey spatial words, such as *above* and *below*.

Informal Assessment

When assessing students' learning, you will need to adapt your expectations of what constitutes an appropriate response. For example, you may wish to have students act out or draw a response to a verbal or written prompt rather than having them give a traditional answer.

Name_____ Date_____

Idea Web

Number each picture to show the order of the steps. Then use time-order words to tell the order of the steps.

How To Make Spaghetti

Step 1, Step 2, Step 3, Step 4

Complete the title. Write or draw what you will explain. Draw pictures to show what to do first, second, third, and fourth. Then show the materials you need in your drawings.

_____

1	2
3	4

Name_____ Date_____

What To Do, What You Need, How To Do It

Write a topic sentence. Tell what you will explain. Then write the materials people need. Write the directions in the right order. Then draw pictures that show the materials and steps.

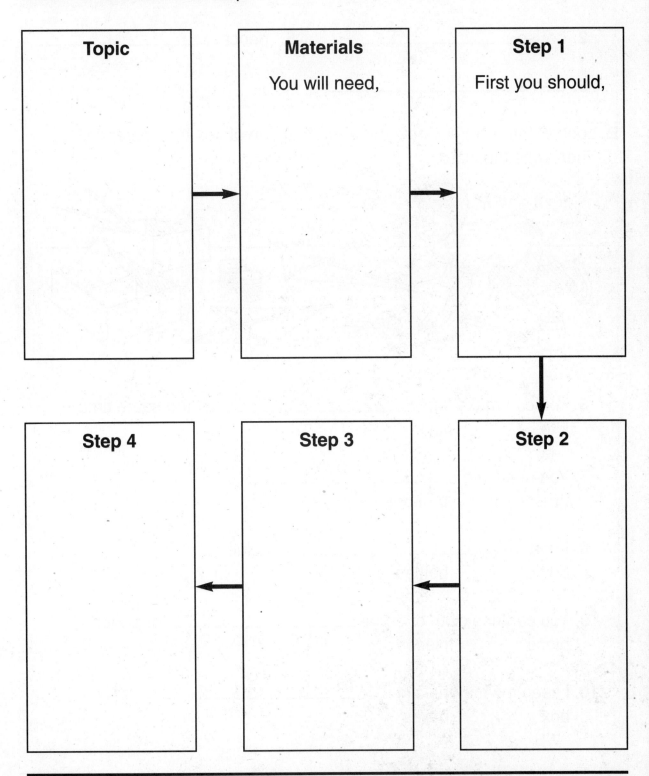

Topic	**Materials** You will need,	**Step 1** First you should,

Step 4	**Step 3**	**Step 2**

Name_____ Date_____

Singular and Plural Nouns

A. Write the plural form of each noun. Add -s or -es.

1. jar _____   **4.** bird _____

2. house _____   **5.** pencil _____

3. dish _____

B. Look at the picture. Circle the noun that completes the sentence. Then write the word.

6. You can make a few _____ at the same time.
   kite   kites

7. You need two _____.
   brush   brushes

8. I use whole _____ of glue.
   bottle   bottles

9. You can use cloth or some _____ of paper.
   piece   pieces

10. I keep my materials in _____.
   box   boxes

I. DEVELOP ORAL LANGUAGE
Oral Focus on Grammar Skill

Objective: Say and write present-tense verb forms.

Whole Group Oral Language Activity

Write *Judy dances.* on the chalkboard and underline *dances.* Say: *An action verb is a word that shows action.* Have students repeat the definition with you. Ask: *What verb in the sentence shows an action?* (dance) Invite a volunteer to act out the word *dances* while the class repeats the verb aloud.

Then explain a present-tense verb tells about an action that takes place now. Say: *The action word* dances *is in the present tense because the action takes place now.*

Teach the three rules on page 162 for forming the present tense with singular subjects. Refer students to the picture on page 160. Write *tune* on the chalkboard and say: *To form the present tense with singular subjects, add –s to most verbs. The boy tunes the guitar.* Have students recite the rule and example sentence with you. Ask: *What is the singular subject?* (boy) Ask a volunteer to come to the chalkboard and add –s to *tune.* Repeat this process for the second and third rules on page 162, using *teach* (The boy teaches guitar.) and *try* (The boy tries a new song.)

Scaffolded Verbal Prompting

Use the following verbal prompts to help students better understand present-tense verbs.

Nonverbal Prompt for Active Participation

Pre-Production: *Act out the sentence as I read it aloud. Raise one arm when you hear the action word.*

One- or Two-Word Response Prompt

Early Production: *Give me a word that tells about an action that takes place now. What letter should I add to the action word if the subject of the sentences is Mike?*

Prompt for Short Answers to Higher-Level Thinking Skills

Speech Emergence: *Read me an action word from the chalkboard. Tell me in a sentence what tense it is.*

Prompt for Detailed Answers to Higher-Level Thinking Skills

Intermediate and Advanced Fluency: *What does the tense of a verb tell? How do you form the present tense of* tune*?*

II. DEVELOP GRAMMAR SKILLS IN CONTEXT
Visual/Physical Focus on Grammar Skill

Objective: Develop and demonstrate understanding of present-tense verbs.

Blackline Master 41

TPR

TPR

Extension: Have students make a list of the verbs suggested by the picture on the cards. Tell students to list them under *–s*, *-es*, and *–ies* endings.

Extension: Challenge students to write sentences using the verbs on the index cards with present-tense endings.

Whole Group Activity

Give each student a copy of Blackline Master 41. Tell students to draw an action on each card whose word has the ending indicated (suggest: jump, crash, carry, and so on). Then students can cut out the cards. Divide the class into two teams. Give each student on team 1 an index card with a present tense verb written on it. Be sure to include verbs that add *-s*, *-es*, and *–ies*. Line up the teams like a spelling bee. Instruct the first student on team 1 to say aloud the verb on the index card and hold it up. Then tell the first student on team 2 to hold up the card that shows the ending needed to form the present tense of that verb. If this students holds up an incorrect card, the next students on team 2 gets a turn. At the half-way point, have teams switch roles.

Small Group Activity

Have students put all their cards from Blackline Master 41 face down on a table. Tell students to take turns turning over a card and naming the present-tense action in the picture drawn there. (The student who drew the picture may need to give a clue.)

Partner Activity

Have partners play the same game described in Whole Group Activity, taking turns presenting index cards and verb ending cards.

Technology Link

Copy a passage from a grade-level book into a word processing program. Change all the verbs to their base forms. Then ask pairs of students to read the passage and change the verbs to the present tense. Students can print their revised passages and exchange papers with other pairs for corrections.

III. PRACTICE GRAMMAR SKILLS
Written Focus on Grammar Skill

Use Blackline Masters 42 and 43 to reinforce adding present-tense endings to verbs.

Introduce Blackline Master 42: Turtles on a Log

Objective: Write and sort present-tense endings.

Materials: Blackline Master 42; glue or paste; pen or pencil

[**Answers**: -s: looks, fills, works; -es: watches, stretches, pushes; -ies: carries, flies, hurries]

Write three list headings on the chalkboard: *-s, -es, -ies*. Refer students to the picture on page 163. Write this cloze sentence: *The big girl _____ at the camera. (smile)* Tell students to give the present-tense form of smile (smiles). Write it in the blank. Then write: *The smaller girl _____ me. (watch)* Tell students to give the present-tense form of watch (watches). Finally, write: *The big girl _____ the smaller girl. (carry)* (carries) Invite volunteers to write the three verbs under the correct ending headings.

Distribute Blackline Master 42. Read aloud and discuss the directions with students. Have students complete the exercise with partners.

Informal Assessment

Read aloud sentences from More Practice on page 161, leaving out the verb. Write the base form of the verb on the chalkboard and ask students to provide the present-tense form.

Introduce Blackline Master 43: Correct the Sentences

Objective: Correct the incorrect present-tense verb forms and identify their singular subjects.

Materials: Blackline Master 43; pen or pencil

[**Answers:** 1. finds, subject: Becky; 2. searches, subject: Fiona; 3. tries, subject: Mark; 4. matches, subject: cape; 5. paints, subject; sister; 6. hurries, subject; Mom]

Write a verb from Blackline Master 42 in a sentence, but put the incorrect present-tense ending on the verb, for example: *This rubberband stretchies wide.* Ask students to correct the verb. Then ask: *What is the singular subject?* (rubberband) Give each student a copy of Blackline Master 43. Help students read and understand the directions as necessary. Have students work with partners or in a small groups to complete the page.

Informal Assessment

From More Practice on page 163, write all the subjects in one column and the base verbs in another column, mixed up. Ask students to tell you the correct present-tense form of each verb and suggest a subject for it (it does not have to be the same subject as in the practice exercise).

Use the following chart to assess and reteach.

Are students able to:	
orally identify verbs in the present tense?	Reteach using the Language Support Activity on TE page 162.
distinguish between the *-s*, *-es*, and *-ies* endings?	Reteach using Reteach BLM 32 on TE page 163.
match present-tense verbs and singular subjects?	Reteach using the Reteach Activity on TE page 163.

s

es

ies

Turtles on a Log

Read the verbs on the turtles. Cut out the turtles and glue or paste them on the log with the right ending.

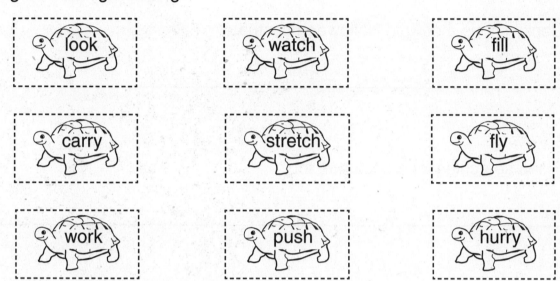

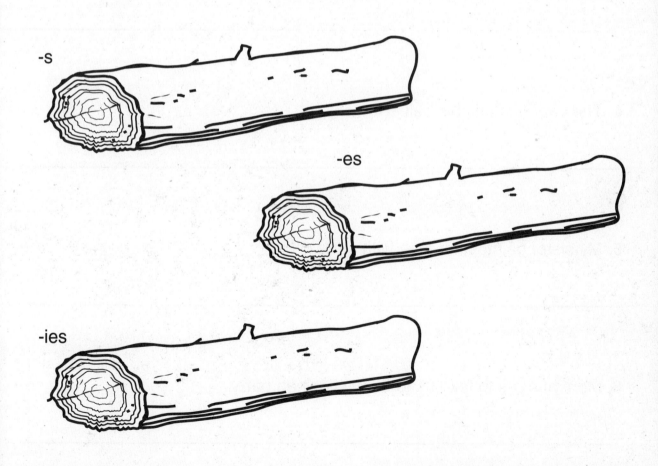

Name_____ Date_____

Correct the Sentences

Read each sentence. Write the sentence with the correct present-tense form of the underlined verb. Circle the singular subject in the sentence you wrote.

1. Becky <u>findes</u> a cowgirl Halloween costume.

_____

2. Fiona <u>searchies</u> for a costume, too.

_____

3. Mark <u>trys</u> on a superman cape.

_____

4. The cape <u>matchs</u> his belt.

_____

5. My sister <u>paintes</u> her face with stars.

_____

6. Mom <u>hurryes</u> to take us to the Halloween party.

_____

SUBJECT-VERB AGREEMENT

I. DEVELOP ORAL LANGUAGE
Oral Focus on Grammar Skill

Objective: Orally recognize that a plural subject agrees with the plural form of the verb; understand the rule for verbs with *you* and *I* as subjects.

Whole Group Oral Language Activity

Elicit that a verb is a word that shows action. Have students look at the picture on page 164. Then write on the chalkboard: *Jim paints the treehouse blue. Ask: What is the singular subject?* (Jim) *What is the present-tense form of paint?* (paints) Explain that the subject agrees with the verb in this sentence.

Now write: *The children paint the treehouse blue.* Ask: *What is the subject?* (The children) *Is it singular or plural?* (plural) Point out that the verb does not have an *–s* ending because the subject is plural, and that the plural subject agrees with the verb. Say: *Do not add –s or –es to a present-tense verb when the subject is plural.* Have students recite this rule with you. Offer similar sentences with *girls/draw* and *animals/play.*

Scaffolded Verbal Prompting

Use the following verbal prompts to help students better understand subject-verb agreement.

Nonverbal Prompt for Active Participation

TPR

Pre-Production: *Raise one hand when I point to a singular subject. Raise two hands when I point to a plural subject. Nod when I point to the correct verb for the singular subject. Stand up when I point to the correct verb for the plural subject.*

One- or Two-Word Response Prompt

Early Production: *What is the subject of (paint)? Say this verb with I and* painters *as the subject. Now say it with* a painter *as the subject. Say it with* you *and* I *as the subject.*

Prompt for Short Answers to Higher-Level Thinking Skills

Speech Emergence: *Tell me the subject and the verb in this sentence. Now can you say the sentence with the subject (you)?*

Prompt for Detailed Answers to Higher-Level Thinking Skills

Intermediate and Advanced Fluency: *How do you know whether or not to add –s or –es to a present-tense verb?*

II. DEVELOP GRAMMAR SKILLS IN CONTEXT
Visual/Physical Focus on Grammar Skill

Objective: Develop and demonstrate understanding of subject-verb agreement

Blackline Master 44

TPR

Whole Group Activity

Distribute copies of Blackline Master 44. Tell students to color the four circles any colors they want and cut them out. Then instruct students to hold their circles and stand in line. On a large piece of display paper, write sentences with singular and plural subjects that do not agree with the verbs *climb* and *catch*. For example: *Dad climb the apple tree. Mom and Dad catches fish.* Ask students to take turns replacing the verbs with one of their circles by pasting it over the incorrect verb. Say the correct sentence together with each student. Then students return to the end of the line and use another circle the next time.

Small Group Activity

Supply groups with a list of singular and plural subjects. Ask students to write as many of these subjects as they can in each circle. Invite group members to read their subjects and verbs aloud to each other.

Partner Activity

Extension: Challenge students to write four sentences using a subject and a verb from each circle.

Partners can write a chant and recite it together, alternating lines. Have them choose from a list of verbs and use each verb with a singular and a plural subject. [a boy chants, many boys chant, I chant, you chant.)

Technology Link

Extension: Pairs of students can take turns leading the class in reciting their chant.

Ask each pair of students to log on to www.mhschool.com/language-arts to find interesting Internet connections about a topic. Have them make a list of the subjects and present-tense verbs they find. Students can print out and share their lists with the class.

III. PRACTICE GRAMMAR SKILLS
Written Focus on Grammar Skill

Use Blackline Masters 45 and 46 to reinforce subject-verb agreement.

Introduce Blackline Master 45: Camping

Objective: Choose the correct subject and verb in parentheses.

Materials: Blackline Master 45; pen or pencil

[**Answers:** 1. likes 2. pitches 3. finds 4. cook 5. rent 6. learn]

Review subject-verb agreement by writing *Animals, squirrel, I,* and *you* on the chalkboard in a list. Give students the verb *climb* and ask them to supply the correct form of the verb for each subject listed. Write their correct responses. Then distribute Blackline Master 45. Read aloud and discuss the directions with students. Have partners complete the page.

Informal Assessment

Go through the sentences in Guided Practice on page 164 with students. After each verb choice, ask students how they know whether to add *–s* or *–es* to a present-tense verb.

Introduce Blackline Master 46: Unscramble the Sentences

Objective: Put sentences in correct word order and identify subjects and verbs that agree.

Materials: Blackline Master 46; pen or pencil

[**Answers:** 1. My brother plays the violin. (arrow from brother to plays); 2. I listen to rock music. (arrow from I to listen); 3. Musicians teach piano lessons. (arrow from Musicians to teach); 4. You learn the oboe. (arrow from You to learn)]

Write this scrambled sentence on the chalkboard: *march in many girls band the.* Ask students to put the words in correct order (Many girls march in the band.) Ask a volunteer to draw an arrow from the subject (girls) to the verb it agrees with (march). Point out that because the subject is plural, we do not add *–es* to the present-tense verb. Give each student a copy of Blackline Master 46. Have them complete the page independently and check their answers with a partner.

Informal Assessment

Say aloud the sentences in More Practice on page 165, omitting the verb. Give students the base form of the verb. Then ask: *What form of the verb belongs in the sentence? Is the subject singular or plural? Is the verb singular or plural? Do they agree?*

Use the following chart to assess and reteach.

Are students able to:	
orally connect subjects and verbs?	Reteach using the Rules box on TE page 164.
make verbs agree with their subjects?	Reteach using the Language Support Activity on TE page 164.
distinguish between singular and plural subjects and verbs?	Reteach using the Reteach Activity on TE page 165.

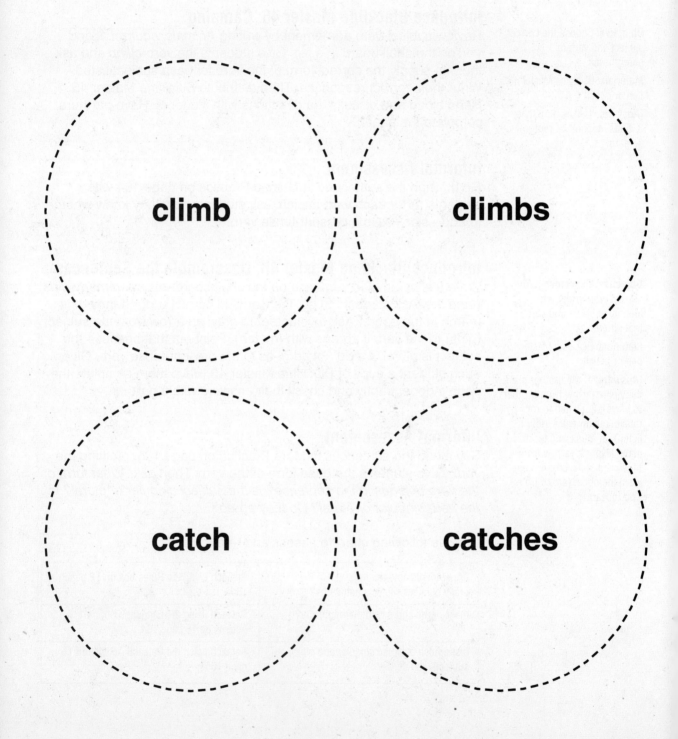

climb

climbs

catch

catches

Camping

Read the sentences and look at the pictures. Circle the correct verb in parentheses.

1. My family (like, likes) camping.

2. My mom (pitch, pitches) our tent in the shade.

3. Dad (find, finds) sticks for a fire.

4. Dad, Mom, and I (cooks, cook) breakfast outside.

5. Mom and Dad (rent, rents) a sailboat on the lake.

6. I (learn, learns) to sail it off the dock.

Unscramble the Sentences

Cut out each word of the sentence. Arrange the words in the correct order and paste them on the lines below. Draw an arrow from the subject to the verb it agrees with.

1.

brother	the	My	plays	violin

2.

music	I	rock	to	listen

3.

piano	teach	lessons	Musicians

4.

learn	oboe	You	the

I. DEVELOP ORAL LANGUAGE
Oral Focus on Grammar Skill

Objective: Compare present- and past-tense verbs.

TPR

Whole Group Oral Language Activity

Write this story on the chalkboard and read it aloud with gestures: *The family cleans the house. Amy dusts all the furniture. Elizabeth mops the kitchen floor. Dad moves the table and chairs. Mom carries the trash outside.* Ask: *How will the story change if the house cleaning happened yesterday?*

Reread each sentence and ask students to supply the past-tense verbs (cleaned, dusted, mopped, moved, carried). Then make four lists on the chalkboard with these headings: *add* –ed, *change* y *to* i *and add* –ed, *drop* e *and add* –ed, *double the consonant and add* –ed. Ask students to help you write the past-tense verbs under the correct heading. As you write each verb, have students read the rule on page 170 aloud with you.

Scaffolded Verbal Prompting

Use the following verbal prompts to help students better understand past-tense verbs.

Nonverbal Prompt for Active Participation

Pre-Production: *Dust your desk now.* Dust *is a verb in the present tense because you are doing the action now. Stop dusting. You dusted your desk.* Dusted *is a verb in the past tense because the action has already happened. Point to the letters I added to the verb* dust *to show past tense.*

One- or Two-Word Response Prompt

Early Production: *What is the past tense of* mop? *Of* dust? *Name the present tense and the past tense of* move.

Prompt for Short Answers to Higher-Level Thinking Skills

Speech Emergence: *What does the past tense show? Read me all the past-tense verbs you see on the chalkboard.*

Prompt for Detailed Answers to Higher-Level Thinking Skills

Intermediate and Advanced Fluency: *How do you know when to use the past tense? Read me this sentence, changing the verb to past-tense.*

II. DEVELOP GRAMMAR SKILLS IN CONTEXT
Visual/Physical Focus on Grammar Skill

Objective: Develop and demonstrate understanding of past-tense verbs

Blackline Master 47

[**Answers:** ripped, hurried, stopped, watched, tried, jumped, hiked, closed]

TPR

TPR

Extension: Have students put away their blackline masters. Give them a list of the past-tense verbs and ask students to write the present-tense forms for singular and plural subjects.

Extension: Challenge partners to write complete sentences using the past-tense verbs and the actions shown in the pictures on Blackline Master 47.

Whole Group Activity

Distribute copies of Blackline Master 47 to students. Give each student a piece of paper to be recycled. Have them rip the paper in half. Write on the chalkboard: *We _____ the paper in half.* Then ask: *What did you do a minute ago?* Write *ripped* in the blank. Have students read the directions to Blackline Master 47 with you and complete number 1 together. For number 2, pantomime hurrying. Write *I _____ across the room.* on the chalkboard. Again ask students what you did a minute ago. Write *hurried* on the line and have students complete number 2 on the blackline master. Then ask volunteers to act out the other verbs in turn and the class to complete the page together.

Small Group Activity

Have students do the whole group activity above in groups of four. Assign two numbers to each student. Monitor as necessary. Have the groups compare their answers.

Partner Activity

Give each partner half of the items on Blackline Master 47 (fold the paper in half). Have partners act out the verbs to each other and complete their half of the page. Partners can then check each other's answers.

Technology Link

Give pairs of students a passage from a book typed into a word processing program. Have them write a list of the past-tense verbs they find. Then have them retype those sentences with the same verbs in present tense. (You may want to do this exercise in reverse and have students look first for present-tense verbs.)

III. PRACTICE GRAMMAR SKILLS
Written Focus on Grammar Skill

Use Blackline Masters 48 and 49 to reinforce using past-tense verbs correctly.

Introduce Blackline Master 48: Verbs in Paint

Draw a flower stem with four large petals on the chalkboard. List these verbs on the chalkboard: *flap, carry, tape, pick.* Point to the first petal and say the rule for adding *–ed* to most verbs to form the past tense. Ask a volunteers to find the verb that fits that rule and write it on that petal (picked). Continue with the other three rules on page 170.

Distribute Blackline Master 48. Read aloud and discuss the directions with students and have them complete the page independently. Partners can check each other's answers.

Objective: Match past-tense verbs to the correct rules.

Materials: Blackline Master 48; pen or pencil, scissors, paste or glue

[**Answers:** add –ed: kick, bump; change y to i and add –ed: spy, cry; drop e and add –ed: wipe, rake; double the consonant and add –ed: tag, plan.]

Informal Assessment

Read aloud the sentences in Guided Practice on page 170, making some verbs past tense and keeping some present tense. Have students tell you which tense you used and give you the other tense.

Introduce Blackline Master 49: Present or Past?

Go back to Blackline Masters 43 and 43. Using some of the sentences, ask students to change the present-tense verbs to past tense and write the new sentences on the chalkboard. Then distribute Blackline Master 49 to each student. Have them complete the page independently and check answers with a partner.

Objective: Identify present and past-tense verbs and write sentences with present and past tense verbs.

Materials: Blackline Master 49; pen or pencil

[**Answers:** 1. Past, plan; 2. Present, traveled; 3. Present, married; 4. Present, danced; 5. Present, missed; 6. Past, walk; 7. Present, collected; 8. Present, grabbed]

Informal Assessment

Have students take turns reading the sentences from More Practice on page 171 and providing the past-tense forms of the verbs.

Use the following chart to assess and reteach.

Are students able to:	
orally identify past-tense verbs?	Reteach using the Language Support Activity on TE page 170.
change the spelling of some verbs in the past tense?	Reteach using Reteach BLM 36 on TE page 171.
use the past tense appropriately?	Reteach using the Reteach Activity on TE page 171.

Match the Verbs

Cut out the past-tense endings. Paste or glue them next to the base form of each verb. Cover up the letters which are no longer needed.

ed	ped	ied	d
ped	d	ed	ied

1. rip _____

2. hurry _____

3. stop _____

4. watch _____

5. try _____

6. jump _____

7. hike _____

8. close _____

Name_____ Date_____

Verbs in Paint

Read the verbs and cut them out. Paste them on the paint palette with the appropriate rule for forming past-tense verbs.

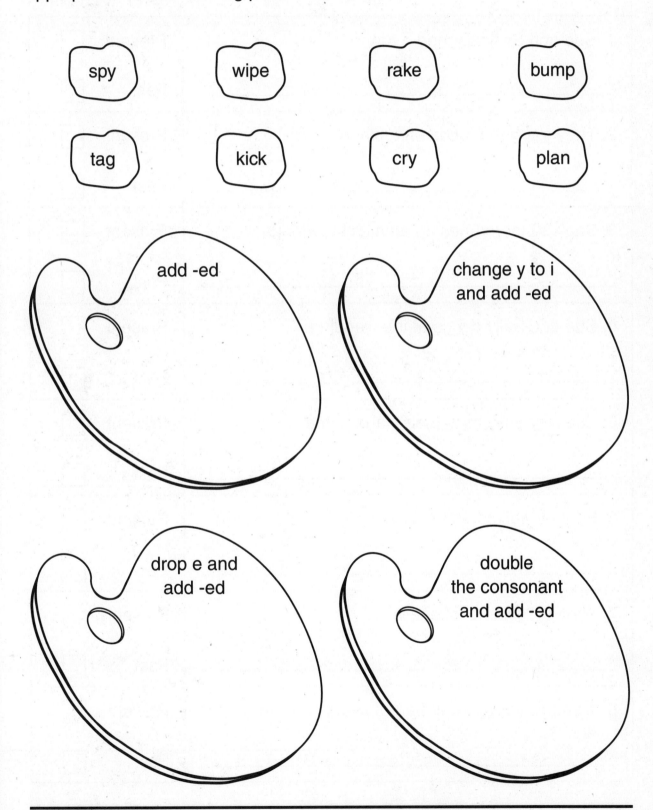

spy

wipe

rake

bump

tag

kick

cry

plan

add -ed

change y to i
and add -ed

drop e and
add -ed

double
the consonant
and add -ed

Name_____ Date_____

Present or Past?

Read each sentence. Check the box that tells the tense of the underlined verb. Write the sentence using the verb in the other tense.

1. Sue and Sally <u>planned</u> a trip. _____	Present ☐ Past ☐
2. They <u>travel</u> to Florida on a plane. _____	Present ☐ Past ☐
3. Sue's sister <u>marries</u> an architect in Florida. _____	Present ☐ Past ☐
4. Sue and Sally <u>dance</u> at the wedding. _____	Present ☐ Past ☐
5. Sue and Sally <u>miss</u> their plane home. _____	Present ☐ Past ☐
6. So they <u>walked</u> on the beach all day. _____	Present ☐ Past ☐
7. They <u>collect</u> a lot of shells. _____	Present ☐ Past ☐
8. A sea gull <u>grabs</u> their bag of shells. _____	Present ☐ Past ☐

I. DEVELOP ORAL LANGUAGE
Oral Focus on Grammar Skill

Objective: Orally identify and classify present, past, and future tense verbs.

TPR

Whole Group Oral Language Activity

Ask a volunteer to face the class. Then tell him to walk slowly in place. Lead the class in describing the volunteer's action. *[Name] walks.* Tell the volunteer to stop. Ask: *What did [Name] do a while ago? [Name] walked a while ago. Tomorrow, I will ask [Name] to walk again. What will he do tomorrow? [Name] will walk.* Write the three sentences on the chalkboard. Call attention to the different forms of the verb *walk*. Ask volunteers to identify the tense of each form. Repeat with other verbs, such as *clap*, *carry*, and *move*.

Then explain that a certain word makes the future tense of most verbs. In the future tense, the action has not happened yet. It is going to happen. Write *will* on the chalkboard. Say it with the first verb in your list (will clap). Have the students give the future tense of all the verbs. Then lead the whole class in reciting the three tenses for each verb.

Scaffolded Verbal Prompting

Use the following verbal prompts to help students better understand future-tense verbs.

Nonverbal Prompt for Active Participation

Pre-Production: *Look at the picture on page 172. Point to the past tense of* sled. *Now point to the future tense of* sled. *Point to the word that makes most verbs future tense* (will).

One- or Two-Word Response Prompt

Early Production: *Say the present, past, and future tenses of (bake). When I say this sentence, tell me what tense the verb is:* The boy sledded down the hill. (past)

Prompt for Short Answers to Higher-Level Thinking Skills

Speech Emergence: *What word makes most verbs future tense?* (will) *Read all the verbs on the chalkboard that are in the future tense. How many words do these verbs have?* (two).

Prompt for Detailed Answers to Higher-Level Thinking Skills

Intermediate and Advanced Fluency: *What does the future tense tell about? How can you tell if a verb is in the future tense? From the chalkboard, read three verbs in the future tense.*

II. DEVELOP GRAMMAR SKILLS IN CONTEXT
Visual/Physical Focus on Grammar Skill

Objective: Develop and demonstrate understanding of future-tense verbs

Materials: Blackline Master 50; scissors

TPR

TPR

Extension: For each verb that students wrote on their cards, have them write the other two tenses.

Extension: Students list the present, past, and future tenses of each verb on the list.

Whole Group Activity

Have students color and cut out the three cards on their own copies of Blackline Master 50. Write a list of base verbs from this unit on the chalkboard. Say: *I'm the verb (paint). I (did this activity yesterday). What tense am I?* Call on a volunteer to stand and hold up the correct card (past) Then have that student write the past-tense form of the verb on the chalkboard. Continue with the other verbs until all students have had a turn.

Small Group Activity

Give each student a list of verbs from this unit, with no duplicates in the lists. Have each student call out a verb from his or her list and use your riddle as a model: I'm the verb (cry). I (will do this activity tomorrow) What tense am I? Students in the group hold up the correct card. Then the student who said the riddle calls on a classmate to write that form of the verb on his or her card. Continue until all students have participated.

Partner Activity

Give students bingo cards with present, past, and future printed on the spaces randomly. Provide partners with a list of base verbs from this unit. One student calls out a verb in one of the three tenses. The other student names the tense and covers the appropriate space with a marker. Students take turns until they both have their bingo cards covered.

Technology Link

Have pairs of students create an electronic master list of present, past, and future tense verbs from this unit. Encourage them to add to the list as they read stories and articles in all subjects.

III. PRACTICE GRAMMAR SKILLS
Written Focus on Grammar Skill

Use Blackline Masters 51 and 52 to reinforce identifying and classifying present, past, and future tense verbs.

Introduce Blackline Master 51: Find the Verbs

Objective: Identify and classify present, past, and future tense verbs.

Materials: Blackline Master 51; pen or pencil

[Answers: present: pick, watch, visit; past; carried, baked, clapped; future: will fix, will give, will go]

Distribute Blackline Master 51. Read aloud and discuss the directions with students. Divide students into small groups to find the nine verbs in the grid and complete the activity. Have groups compare their lists.

Informal Assessment

Read aloud sentences from Guided Practice on page 172 and More Practice on page 173, omitting the verbs. Have students provide the future-tense verbs.

Introduce Blackline Master 52: Three Tenses

Objective: Write the correct tense of the verb.

Materials: Blackline Master 52; pen or pencil

[Answers: 1. will play; 2. finished; 3. wants; 4. will call; 5. will clean; 6. help; 7. watches; 8. will visit]

Write on the chalkboard a few sentences from Guided Practice or More Practice in this unit. Give the base form of the verb and indicate present, past, or future tense. Ask volunteers to provide the correct answers and write them on the chalkboard. The give each student a copy of Blackline Master 52. After you read the directions, have students work in pairs to complete the exercise.

Informal Assessment

Have students complete these sentences:

A _____ _____ verb tells about an action that is going to happen.

A _____ _____ verb tells what happens now.

A _____ _____ verb tells about an action that has already happened.

The word _____ usually indicates future tense.

Use the following chart to assess and reteach.

Are students able to:	
orally identify future-tense verbs?	Reteach using the Language Support Activity on TE page 172.
use *will* to make the future tense?	Reteach using the Rules box on page 172.
use the future tense appropriately?	Reteach using the Reteach Activity on TE page 173.

present

past

future

Find the Verbs

Find and circle the nine verbs in the grid. Write the verbs in the correct lists on the lines below.

w	p	r	e	e	w	x	b
a	i	v	i	s	i	t	a
t	c	l	w	w	l	w	k
c	k	q	l	q	l	b	e
h	b	x	b	g	f	b	d
d	c	a	r	r	i	e	d
s	s	g	g	u	x	v	u
c	l	a	p	p	e	d	e
h	h	a	c	c	s	u	u
w	i	l	l	g	o	f	f

present   past   future

_____   _____   _____

_____   _____   _____

_____   _____   _____

Three Tenses

Write each sentence. Use the verb in parentheses in the tense named.

1. I (play, future) computer games after school.

_____

2. I (finish, past) my homework last night.

_____

3. My Mom (want, present) me to clean my room soon.

_____

4. First, I (call, future) my best friend on the phone.

_____

5. Then I (clean, future) my room.

_____

6. I (help, present) with dinner every night.

_____

7. My sister (watch, present) TV before dinner.

_____

8. We (visit, future) my grandmother later.

_____

PREFIXES

Introduce this lesson before Pupil Edition pages 190–191.

I. DEVELOP ORAL LANGUAGE
Oral Focus on Vocabulary Skill

Objective: Identify and use prefixes *dis-*, *un-*, and *re-*.

TPR

Whole Group Oral Language Activity

Write the words *appear, disappear,* and *reappear* on the chalkboard. Explain that we can add prefixes to the beginning of words to change their meaning. Discuss the meaning of *dis-* (not, the opposite of) and *re-* (again, back). Ask a volunteer to act out the sequence as you and the class say the words *appear, disappear,* and *reappear.*

Repeat the same process as you lock, unlock, and relock a door. Review the prefix *un-* and its meanings (not, the opposite of).

Scaffolded Verbal Prompting

Use the following verbal prompts to help students better understand words with prefixes *dis-*, *un-*, and *re-* and their meanings.

Nonverbal Prompt for Active Participation
TPR

Pre-Production: Say: *Raise your hand if I say a word that has the prefix* dis-, un-, *or* re-. *Put your hand down if the word I say doesn't have one of these prefixes.* Say: *untie, undo, unite, disagree, direct.*

One- or Two-Word Response Prompt

Early Production: *Name the prefix in the word dislike. (dis-)*

Prompt for Short Answers to Higher-Level Thinking Skills

Speech Emergence: *Name a word that means not true. (untrue)*

Prompt for Detailed Answers to Higher-Level Thinking Skills

Intermediate and Advanced Fluency: *Tell how you know what the word* rewrite *means. Then use the word in a sentence.*

II. DEVELOP VOCABULARY SKILLS IN CONTEXT
Visual/Physical Focus on Vocabulary Skill

Objective: Identify words with prefixes *dis-*, *un-*, and *re-*

Small Group Activity

Write the following words on the chalkboard: *fold, fair, zip, plug, aware, button, hook, happy, approve, appear, honest, able, order, place, wind, build, load, open, check, enter,* and *view.* Have groups brainstorm words for a prefix word wall listing words with the same prefix together.

Technology Link

Show students how to use electronic dictionaries on CD-ROM or on the Internet. Then ask pairs of students to find words with the prefixes *dis-*, *un-*, and *re-* and to check their meanings.

Partner Activity

Prepare a set of cards for each pair of students. On each card write a word with a prefix *dis-*, *un-*, or *re*. The words you choose should be ones that can be acted out, such as *disappoint, unfold, unbutton, rebuild,* and *reenter.* Give partners a set of cards. Have partners mix up the cards and place them face down on the table. Have one partner take a card and read the word silently. The partner can tell the other partner only the prefix of the word he/she will act out. Then have the partner act out the word and have the other partner name the word.

TPR

III. PRACTICE VOCABULARY SKILLS
Written Focus on Vocabulary Skill

Objective: Identify the word with *dis, un-,* or *re-* that matches a drawing

Materials: Blackline Master 53; pencils

[Answers: 1: reread; 2: disagree; 3: unhappy; 4: disconnect; 5: rebuild; 6: unhook; 7: repay; 8: unopened; 9: disordered]

Introduce Blackline Master 53: Find the Prefix

Distribute Blackline Master 53. Review the prefixes *dis-*, *un-*, and *re-* and their meanings. Read the directions with students and work through the first exercise with them. Ask volunteers to read the two words below the first picture. Then ask students which word tells what the boy is doing. (reread) Discuss what each word means. Have students circle the word that shows what the boy is doing. Check students' responses. Then have them complete the exercises.

Introduce Blackline Master 54: Write Prefixes

Distribute Blackline Master 54. Read the directions with students and ask a volunteer to read the first definition. Then write *diswise, unwise,* and *rewise* on the chalkboard. Read the words with students. Discuss which is the real word that matches the meaning *not wise.* Instruct students to write the correct prefix on the line. Check students' work. Have students complete the rest of the exercises independently.

Objective: Associate prefixes dis-, un-, and re- with their meanings

Materials: Blackline Master 54; pencils

[Answers: 1: unwise; 2: displeased; 3: rewind; 4: disagree; 5: uncut; 6: dishonest; 7: resend; 8: unpacked; 9: recall; 10: disappear]

Informal Assessment

Have students turn to page 191 in the textbook. Refer them to exercise one in Practice A. Ask, *What does the prefix re- mean in the word* reread? Next, read aloud exercise 7 in Practice B. Ask, *How do you know what the word* unable *means?* (Unable *has the prefix* un- *which means* not. *So* unable *means* not able.)

Use the following chart to assess and reteach.

Are students able to: change the meaning of a word by adding a prefix?	Reteach using the Language Support activity on TE page 190.
identify words made with prefixes dis-, un-, and re- and identify their meanings?	Reteach using the Reteach Activity on TE page 191.

Find the Prefix

Look at each picture. Read the two words below each picture. Circle the word with the prefix that names the picture.

1.

reread   reach

2.

disk   disagree

3.

unite   unhappy

4.

disconnect   different

5.

rebuild   read

6.

under   unhook

7.

real   return

8.

unopened   uncle

9.

dipper   disordered

Write Prefixes

Read each definition. Write the prefix from the box to make the word match the meaning.

dis-	un-	re-

1. not wise: _____ wise

2. the opposite of pleased: _____ pleased

3. wind again: _____ wind

4. the opposite of agree: _____ agree

5. not cut: _____ cut

6. not honest: _____ honest

7. send again: _____ send

8. the opposite of packed: _____ packed

9. call back: _____ call

10. the opposite of appear: _____ appear

LEADS AND ENDINGS

Introduce this lesson before Pupil Edition pages 192-193.

I. DEVELOP ORAL LANGUAGE
Oral Focus on Composition Skill

Objective: Orally describe a picture using a strong lead.

Whole Group Oral Language Activity

Show students a news photograph of a local or national event. Ask them what is happening in the photo. Tell them that a news article always begins with a strong lead. The lead is the first sentence. Ask: *If you were reading a news article and the first sentence—the lead— wasn't interesting, what would you do?* Lead students to see that as strong lead is important because it gets the reader's attention. If they don't get the reader's attention, the reader may stop reading. Have students work together to brainstorm possible leads for the story to accompany the news photo. Decide on the three best ones, and let students vote for the one they like best.

Scaffolded Verbal Prompting

Use the following verbal prompts to help students understand the importance of a strong lead.

Nonverbal Prompt for Active Participation

TPR

Pre-Production: Show students a photo in the classroom, or supply a photo from a magazine or newspaper. *Show me what someone in the photo is doing.*

One- or Two-Word Response Prompt

Early Production: Use the same photo. *Tell who is in the picture. What are they doing?*

Prompt for Short Answers to Higher-Level Thinking Skills

Speech Emergence: *Tell in a sentence what is happening in the photo.*

Prompt for Detailed Answers to Higher-Level Thinking Skills

Intermediate and Advanced Fluency: *Look at the picture. If you were writing the story to go with it, how would you start your story?*

Extension: Ask students to write a news story to go with the picture.

II. DEVELOP COMPOSITION SKILLS IN CONTEXT
Visual/Physical Focus on Composition Skill

Objective: Come up with a cooperative story to describe a photograph, using a strong lead and ending.
TPR

Small Group Activity

Form students into groups. Give each group a different photograph. Ask them to work together to think of a story that tells about it. Tell them to think of a strong lead sentence. Then remind them that the ending should sum up the story, restate the main idea, or tell something they have learned about the topic. Have groups take turns telling their story.

Technology Link

Have each group type their lead into the computer. If possible, scan the photo into the computer, too. If not, number the photo and number the story lead to correspond. Allow all the students to add their ideas for the story to the lead.

Partner Activity

Make picture cards, using cutouts from magazines glued to index cards. Have each pair select a picture card at random. Then have them work together to come up with a good lead and a good ending for a story to go along with the picture.

Extension: Have students, working in pairs, complete their stories about the pictures they've chosen. Ask them to come up with a good headline.

III. PRACTICE COMPOSITION SKILLS
Written Focus on Composition Skill

Introduce Blackline Master 55: Lead On

Form student pairs of varying language proficiency levels. Distribute copies of Blackline Master 55 to all students. Read the directions aloud with students, and review what goes into making a lead a strong one. Have pairs work together to come up with their leads. After students have finished, have them share their leads with other pairs.

Objective: Write a strong lead for a story to go along with a picture.

Materials: Blackline Master 55; pencil

[Answers will vary. Examples: *1. There was a close race today. 2. A local dog may have found pirates' treasure!*]

Introduce Blackline Master 56: Beginning or End

Distribute Blackline Master 56 to each student. Read the directions aloud, and review some of the characteristics of leads and endings. Work through the first item with students. When everyone has finished, go over the sheet together. Help students who chose the wrong answer to figure out why their answers are incorrect.

Objective: To identify leads and endings.

Materials: Blackline Master 56; pencil

[**Answers:** 1. Ending, 2. Lead, 3. Ending, 4. Lead, 5. Ending, 6. Lead, 7. Ending, 8. Ending]

Informal Assessment

Have students turn to page 193 in their textbooks. Refer them to Blackline Master 55, item 4. Ask whether that sentence would make a good lead or a good ending.

Assess and Reteach

Is the student able to: write leads that catch the reader's attention?	Reteach by allowing pre- and early production students to pantomime or draw their responses.
identify leads and endings?	Reteach using the Reteach Activity on TE page 193.

Name_____ Date_____

Lead On

Look at each picture. On the lines next to it, write a good lead for a story to go along with the picture.

_____
_____
_____
_____
_____
_____
_____

_____
_____
_____
_____
_____

Beginning or End?

Read each sentence. Decide whether it is a lead or an ending. Circle **Lead** or **Ending** after each sentence.

1. After all, I'm happy everything happened the way it did.   **Lead**   **Ending**

2. Would you like to learn more about worms?   **Lead**   **Ending**

3. Finally, we fell asleep, happy and tired.   **Lead**   **Ending**

4. The big parade starts today at 12 noon!   **Lead**   **Ending**

5. When we had finished looking, we found the watch right on the table!   **Lead**   **Ending**

6. Jen Ling will give a piano recital Thursday at Swaim Hall.   **Lead**   **Ending**

7. We can't wait to go again!   **Lead**   **Ending**

8. That was the last time we ever saw Old Slither, the snake.   **Lead**   **Ending**

Introduce this lesson before Pupil Edition pages 202–217

I. PREWRITE
Oral Warm Up

Objectives:
• Identify facts and opinions.
• Give and generate reasons for opinions.

Whole Group Oral Language Activity

Display a handful of crayons in different colors. Hold up the crayons one at a time and ask: *Is this a (blue) crayon?* Use the responses to review that a fact is a statement that is true. Then say: *If we could paint our room in any color, I feel we should paint it blue.* Ask students to agree or disagree. Using their responses as examples, review that an opinion is what someone thinks or believes.

Explain that people give reasons for their opinions to try to persuade or convince people that their opinions are good ideas. Ask: *Do you think our playground needs a basketball hoop?* Write a chart labeled Opinion and Reasons. Fill it in with volunteers' responses.

Graphic Organizer

Blackline Master 57

Objectives:
• Use a graphic organizer to give and support an opinion
• Practice persuasive writing

Materials: Blackline Master 57; pencils, crayons

Introduce the Writing Mode

Explain that people use persuasive writing to convince people that their ideas are worth considering. They use opinions and facts to persuade people. Model persuasive writing about painting your classroom. (Example: *We should choose the colors of our classrooms. Yellow walls would make people feel happy and warm. Classrooms would be easy to find if they were painted different colors. The rooms are painted every year, so it wouldn't cost extra money.*)

Pre-Production and Early Production

TPR

Speech Emergence

Intermediate and Advanced Fluency

Scaffolded Writing Instruction

Using Blackline Master 57, have students give an opinion about what color the classroom should be or what the classroom needs, by drawing or coloring. Then have them draw a picture to show three reasons they could give to persuade others about their opinion.

Have students draw and/or color. Encourage them to write words and phrases to accompany each drawing.

Have students draw or color the top box and write a sentence that gives their opinion. Then have them create sentences that give three reasons for their opinions in the remaining boxes.

Research and Inquiry: Note Taking Using Library Sources

Explain that libraries have newspapers and magazines that contain facts that students can include in their persuasive writing. Using a magazine article that students may be interested in, read the title and the first paragraph. Ask students to take notes.

II. DRAFT

Objectives:
- Organize ideas for persuasive writing
- Begin drafting a persuasive paragraph

TPR

Focus on Explanatory Writing

Model how to begin a persuasive paragraph by stating an opinion. Write the following idea on the board and read it aloud: *Our class needs a world map. We only have a map of The United States. A world map would help us discuss other countries. Many students know about other places and could help us learn about them.* Ask a volunteer to underline the opinion in the paragraph, and to draw two lines under the sentences that give reasons for the opinion.

Have students brainstorm opinions about something they wish their school had or how the school could be improved and list them on the chalkboard. Ask volunteers to give reasons that support each topic. Discuss students' reasons and examine whether or not they are persuasive. For example: *I think we should have a swimming pool.* Then discuss with students which of the following is the better reason: *I like to swim,* or *Children need to learn how to swim.*

Scaffolded Writing Instruction

Pre-Production
Early Production
Blackline Master 58

Use Blackline Master 58 to help students organize their persuasive reasons. Have them draw or cut out and paste pictures that identify their opinion and three reasons that support it.

Speech Emergence
Blackline Master 59

Using Blackline Master 59, guide students to draw and write words and phrases to state their opinion and to give three reasons that will help persuade the principal of their school to support their opinions. Encourage students to state a fact as one of their reasons.

Intermediate and Advanced
Fluency

Students may begin to write a persuasive paragraph. Have students write one sentence stating their opinion, and one or two sentences in each box that states a reason.

III. REVISE

Objectives:
- Revise persuasive writing
- Add facts and reasons that support an opinion

TPR

Focus on Elaboration

Explain that some words and phrases can help them discuss their ideas. Write the following words and phrases on the board: *I think, I believe, we should, we could.* Ask volunteers to refer to their drafts and read or act out one of their reasons, first using one of these phrases.

Point to the sentence you wrote: *Many students know about other places and could help us learn about them.* Explain that you could make your reason more convincing by adding details. Write and say the following sentences: *We have students from (country) and (country). If we had a map, our students could help us learn about these places.* On the chalkboard write other reasons and add details elicited from students.

Scaffolded Instruction for Revising

Pre-Production and Early
Production
Blackline Master 58

Speech Emergence
Blackline Master 59

Intermediate and Advanced
Fluency

Have students revise their work in Blackline Master 58 by drawing or adding details.

Use students' work on Blackline Master 59 to help them add details to make their reasons stronger. Have them add some of the idea phrases from the chalkboard where appropriate.

Students may elaborate by adding specific details that make their reasons more convincing and by adding some of the idea phrases on the chalkboard. Encourage students to write a concluding sentence that restates their opinion in a slightly different way.

Technology Link

Have partners use a computer to choose a font that is easy to read. Have them type in their list of reasons, highlight them, then choose a font under Font in the Format menu, and select a type size that is 12 points or higher.

IV. REVISE • PEER CONFERENCING

Focus on Peer Conferencing

Objectives:
• Participate in peer conferences
• Give and receive suggestions for improvement
• Revise persuasive writing

Pair students of similar fluency levels. Pre-production and early production students should interpret their drawings for partners by gesturing or acting out their opinions and then their reasons. Have partners brainstorm an additional reason that will help persuade readers. Emerging speakers should help partners add idea and opinion words. Encourage fluent speakers to question whether there are unneeded sentences, repeated ideas, or sentences that give non-persuasive reasons.

Using page 210 as a guide, write and read a checklist for each language proficiency level on the chalkboard, so students can refer to them as they hold their peer conferences.

V. PROOFREAD

Focus on English Conventions

Objectives:
• Demonstrate comprehension of proofreading strategies.
• Use present-tense and past-tense verbs.

Remind students that a present-tense verb shows that an action is happening now, or in the present. A past-tense verb tells about an action that happened in the past, or before now. Say and write the following sentences:
> I like the principal. They liked the principal.
> He wished they had a garden. She wishes they had a garden.

Ask a volunteer to underline the present-tense verb in each sentence pair. Have another student underline the past-tense verbs twice. Explain that many verbs form the past tense by adding -d or -ed to the present tense of the verb. Discuss that when students proofread their work, they can look for mistakes with verb tenses.

Blackline Master 60
Objective: Use past-tense and present-tense verbs.
[**Answers: A.** 1. wants, 2. clapped, 3. decided, 4. hope, 5. reads, **B.** 1. learned, 2. wished, 3. searched, 4. saved, 5. turned]

Spelling Tip
Have students begin a personal word file. Have them write words they have trouble spelling on index cards. They can arrange the cards in alphabetical order.

Have students complete Blackline Master 60 to practice the grammar skill. Ask students to reread their sentences to make sure that they have used past-tense and present-tense verbs correctly.

List words that are commonly used in letters. Point out that each of the words begins with a capital letter and that the abbreviations end with a period. Encourage students to use the list as they proofread their work: *Mr., Mrs., Ms., Dear, Sincerely, (name of present month).*

Help students use spatial reasoning to begin to locate words in a dictionary. Ask a student to open the dictionary in the middle. Ask what letter the words on the page begin with. Point out that the first half of the alphabet includes letters from a–m. The second half includes the letters n–z. Then have the student turn to nearby pages to find words that begin with -n.

VI. PUBLISH

Objective: Present a persuasive letter as a speech.

Use page 136 as a guide and write and read aloud a checklist for each language proficiency level. Encourage students to use the checklist as they prepare their speeches.

Give a Speech

Extension: Adapt the suggestions on page 216–217 to generate activities that will bring out the talents of students at all proficiency levels.

Tell students that people often read their letters aloud at public meetings. Place students into mixed language-level groups to share their writing and decide on an order of presentation. Students who drew pictures may ask more fluent speakers to write headings to create a letter format. All students should collaborate to create strong first-sentence opinions for their letters.

VII. LISTENING, SPEAKING, VIEWING, REPRESENTING

Encourage ESL students to point to elements in their pictures as they speak and to hold up their fingers to indicate reasons "one, two, three." Invite them to substitute words in their native languages if they cannot convey their meaning in English.

Informal Assessment

When assessing students' learning, you will need to adapt your expectations of what constitutes an appropriate response. For example, you may wish to have students act out or draw a response.

My Opinion/Why?

Decide on your opinion about the color of the walls in the room. Color or draw to show your opinion. Then draw or write three reasons why people should agree.

My Idea

Why?

1.

2.

3.

My Opinion, My Reasons

Think about what your school needs. Draw a picture of your opinion in the think bubble. Then draw three reasons that will convince other people.

My Opinion

My Reasons

1.

2.

3.

Name_____ Date_____

Opinion and Reasons

Fill in the date and the greeting. Write or draw your opinion about what the school needs. Use words, phrases, and sentences to give your reasons. Then draw pictures to help support your ideas.

(Month and Day) _____ (Year) _____

Dear _____,

(Opinion) I think

(Reason)

(Reason)

(Reason)

Sincerely,

(Name) _____

Name_____ Date_____

Present-Tense and Past-Tense Verbs

A. Circle the verb that belongs in the sentence. Then write the word.

1. Shana says she _____ new swings for the playground.

    wants   wanted

2. Everybody _____ when she read her letter.

    claps   clapped

3. The principal _____ that swings were dangerous.

    decides   decided

4. I _____ he will change his mind.

    hope   hoped

5. He always _____ our letters.

    reading   reads

B. Write the past-tense form of each word. Add *-d* or *-ed*.

Present Tense   **Past Tense**

1. learn   _____

2. wish   _____

3. search   _____

4. save   _____

5. turn   _____

MAIN AND HELPING VERBS

I. DEVELOP ORAL LANGUAGE
Oral Focus on Grammar Skill

Objective: Distinguish between main and helping verbs.

TPR

Whole Group Oral Language Activity

Review how verbs tell what the subject does or is doing in a sentence. Ask volunteers to give examples of verbs. Then direct students to the photograph on page 242 of the textbook. Tell them the children at the party are playing a game where they act out verbs. Write this sentence on the chalkboard: *Milone is jumping across the room.* Draw a circle around *is* and underline *jumping.* Prompt a volunteer to show the action. Invite students to describe the action. Then guide students to read first the helping verb, then the main verb, and finally the sentence aloud with you.

Using the chart on page 240, ask volunteers to name a main verb for each helping verb. Explain that the verbs *is, am,* and *are* help the main verb show an action that is going on now. Then point out that the verbs *was* and *were* help the main verb show an action that was going on in the past. Also explain that the verbs *have, has, had* help the main verb show past action and that the verb *will* helps the main verb show future action. Demonstrate the concept by asking two volunteers to act out this sentence: *Jim and Ella are walking.* Ask: *What are Jim and Ella doing now?* Tell the volunteers to stop. Then ask: *What were Jim and Ella doing a while ago? What have they done? What will they do tomorrow?* Repeat the demonstration using singular subjects.

Scaffolded Verbal Prompting

Use the following verbal prompts to help students better understand main and helping verbs.

Nonverbal Prompt for Active Participation

Pre-Production: *Point to a helping verb in a sentence on the chalkboard. Now point to a main verb. Show me the action of the whole verb.*

One- or Two-Word Response Prompt

Early Production: *Tell me a helping verb you see on the chalkboard. Now tell me a main verb. Say the whole verb. Next, say the main verb with a different helping verb.*

Prompt for Short Answers to Higher-Level Thinking Skills

Speech Emergence: *Read me a sentence from the chalkboard with the helping verb* has *in it. What is the main verb in that sentence? Now read a sentence with the helping verb* will. *What is the main verb in that sentence?*

Prompt for Detailed Answers to Higher-Level Thinking Skills

Intermediate and Advanced Fluency: *Tell me in a complete sentence what the main verb does. What does the helping verb do?*

II. DEVELOP GRAMMAR SKILLS IN CONTEXT
Visual/Physical Focus on Grammar Skill

Objective: Develop and demonstrate understanding of main and helping verbs.

Materials: Blackline Master 61; crayons

TPR

Extension: Invite students to write and illustrate sentences using the verbs. They can make a class picture dictionary of main and helping verbs.

Whole Group Activity

Make a list of several main and helping verbs on the chalkboard, such as *is cleaning, are working, has mowed, will scrub.* Give each student a copy of Blackline Master 61. Tell them to color the *main verb* card green, the *helping verb* card yellow, the *form of have* card purple, and the *form of be* card orange. Then instruct students to cut out the cards.

Divide the class in half. Point to a main verb in the list on the chalkboard and say to students on one side of the room: *Raise the card that tells what kind of verb this is.* Have students say the verb with you. Then point to a helping verb and do the same with students on the other side of the room. Next, point again to the helping verb and ask the whole class to raise the *have* or *be* card. Prompt students to say the whole verb with you. Invite a volunteer to act out the verb. Repeat with other verbs and alternate sides of the room.

Small Group Activity

Copy the list of verbs from the chalkboard for each group of four students. Have them use the cards from Blackline Master 61 as list headings and write the verbs in the appropriate lists. Tell students that verbs will belong in more than one list. For example, *is* is a form of *be* and a helping verb.

Partner Activity

Have partners quiz each other on main and helping verbs, using the list on the chalkboard. One student asks: What kind of verb is *has?* The other student writes the answer on the back of the appropriate card from Blackline Master 61. Pairs of students exchange their cards with another pair and check each other's work.

Technology Link

Copy a paragraph from a book into a word processing program. Ask partners of different language levels to cut and paste the main and helping verbs into a list.

III. PRACTICE GRAMMAR SKILLS
Written Focus on Grammar Skill

Use the following Blackline masters to reinforce unit grammar skills.

Introduce Blackline Master 62: Match Subjects and Irregular Verbs

Objective: Match singular and plural subjects with irregular verbs and write sentences with the form of the verb indicated.

Materials: Blackline Master 62; pen or pencil

[**Answers:** 1. Draw a line connecting *He* with the third picture. 2. Draw a line connecting *They* to the first picture. 3. Draw a line connecting *She* to the second picture.]

Give students practice making the helping verb agree with the subject of a sentence. Write on the chalkboard: *He (mix; past with a form of have) the cookie dough.* Ask: *What past form of have do we use with the singular subject he?* (has) Write *has* above the parentheses. Then ask: *What is the main verb form of mix after has?* (mixed) Write *mixed* above the parentheses. Have students read the complete sentence aloud with you.

Distribute copies of Blackline Master 62. Work through the first item with students if necessary. Have partners complete the page.

Informal Assessment

Refer to the rule and example chart on page 242. For each sentence in the Example column, ask students to tell you whether the subject is singular or plural and to name the main and helping verb.

Introduce Blackline Master 63: Make Up Irregular Verb Sentences

Objective: Combine subjects, helping verbs, and main verbs in original sentences.

Materials: Blackline Master 63; pen or pencil

[Answers will vary.]

Write the subject *She* on the chalkboard. Ask students to call out any helping verb that goes with a singular subject. *(is, has)* Then ask students to think of a main verb, for example, *fix* or *wash*. Write the verbs on the chalkboard next to the subject. Prompt students to provide the correct form of the main verb *(She is fixing)*. Finally, ask students to think of a way to finish the sentence. (She is fixing a party snack.)

Give each student a copy of Blackline Master 63. Guide students in writing the first sentence as necessary. Then tell students to complete the page on their own and check their work with a partner.

Informal Assessment

Review sentences in More Practice on page 243 with students. Ask students to name the subjects and tell you if they are singular or plural.

Use the following chart to assess and reteach.

Are students able to:	
orally identify main and helping verbs?	Reteach using the Language Support Activity on TE page 240.
combine main and helping verbs correctly?	Reteach using the Language Support Activity on TE page 243.
use singular and plural subjects with the correct helping verbs?	Reteach using the Language Support Activity on TE page 242.

Main verb

Helping verb

Form of *have*

Form of *be*

Match Subjects and Irregular Verbs

Read the subject of the sentence in the first column. Draw a line to the correct verb in parentheses and picture. Write the whole sentence with a correct form of the verb on the numbered line below.

1. He	(measure; past with form of *have*)
2. They	(taste; present with form of *be*)
3. She	(chop; past with form of *have*)

1. _____

2. _____

3. _____

Make Up Irregular Verb Sentences

Read the words in the chart. Choose any subjects and main and helping verbs that go together. Make up sentences using them on the lines below.

Subject	Helping verb	Main verb
They	has	bring
He	are	throw
She	was	watch
You	had	taste

1. _____

2. _____

3. _____

4. _____

IRREGULAR AND MORE IRREGULAR VERBS

I. DEVELOP ORAL LANGUAGE
Oral Focus on Grammar Skill

Objective: Explain how irregular verbs change their spelling.

Whole Group Oral Language Activity

Ask students to look at the photograph on page 253. Ask: *What do you think the man did yesterday?* Prompt responses that include irregular verbs, such as *He sang a cowboy song. He had eaten lunch before he sang. He went on a long ride.* Write the irregular verbs on the chalkboard.

Explain that these verbs have a change in spelling for the past tense and the past with *have, has,* or *had.* Write the three forms on the chalkboard *(sing, sang, sung; eat, ate, eaten; go, went, gone).* Have students say and spell them aloud with you. Then name a verb and a tense *(eat, past)* and ask volunteers to call out the correct verb *(ate).*

Scaffolded Verbal Prompting

Use the following verbal prompts to help students better understand irregular verbs.

Nonverbal Prompt for Active Participation

Pre-Production: *Look at the verbs on the chalkboard. Point to a present tense verb. Now point to the form for past with* have, has, *or* had.

One- or Two-Word Response Prompt

Early Production: *Say a past-tense verb that you see on the chalkboard. Now say its form in the present tense. Tell me what's special about the spelling of irregular verbs.* (it changes)

Prompt for Short Answers to Higher-Level Thinking Skills

Speech Emergence: *What are all the past with* have, has, *or* had *forms on the chalkboard? Name all the present tense forms. What letter in the verb sing changes in the past tenses?*

Prompt for Detailed Answers to Higher-Level Thinking Skills

Intermediate and Advanced Fluency: *Explain in one sentence how the spelling of* eat *changes in the past tenses. Now explain the changes in spelling for* go.

II. DEVELOP GRAMMAR SKILLS IN CONTEXT
Visual/Physical Focus on Grammar Skill

Objective: Develop and demonstrate understanding of irregular verbs.

Blackline Master 64

TPR

Extension: Have partners say or write three sentences, with a different verb for each tense.

Whole Group Activity

Make a three-column chart on the chalkboard like the one on page 252. Write *do* in the first column. Provide each student with a copy of Blackline Master 64. Ask students to look at the list of verbs and point to or call out the past tense of *do (did)*. Instruct students to cut out that verb and paste or glue it into the second column of the chart as you write it on the chalkboard. Continue with the rest of the verb forms.

Small Group Activity

Give each group a set of cards with the present, present past, and past with *have, has,* or *had* forms of three irregular verbs, one verb per card. Divide the cards equally among students. As you call out a verb and a tense, ask students with that verb card to stand up and stretch, then set the card aside. Call out verbs until each group has identified each verb. Then ask groups to arrange their cards in piles by verb tense.

Partner Activity

Give partners sets of cards with irregular verbs in three tenses. Have one student say a verb and the other student name the other two forms. Then have students switch roles.

Technology Link

In a word processing program, make an irregular verb exercise for students. Create a chart with the three forms of several irregular verbs. Mix up the verbs so some of them are in the wrong places. Ask students to arrange the verbs correctly with the cut and paste function.

III. PRACTICE GRAMMAR SKILLS
Written Focus on Grammar Skill

Use the following Blackline masters to reinforce unit grammar skills.

Introduce Blackline Master 65: Verb Pictures

Objective: Choose the picture that represents the correct verb and write the verb form.

Materials: Blackline Master 65; scissors; paste or glue; pen or pencil

[**Answers:** Present: run, Past: ate; Past with *have, has,* or *had:* said, sang]

Distribute Blackline Master 65. Read aloud and discuss the directions with students. Ask: *What is happening in these pictures?* Explain that the actions in the pictures will complete the verb chart. Work through one exercise together. Ask pairs to complete the rest.

Informal Assessment

Use sentences from More Practice on page 253. Read a sentence aloud without the verb. Write the present tense of the verb on the chalkboard and ask: *What is the correct form? What tense is that?* Write the tense next to the verb. Then read the sentence with the verb and have students repeat it.

Introduce Blackline Master 66: Write Irregular Verbs

Objective: Provide the correct form of the irregular verb to complete each sentence.

Materials: Blackline Master 66; pen or pencil

[**Answers:** went, gave, ate, sang, said, ran, had seen, had eaten]

Write this sentence on the chalkboard and read it with students: The Fourth of July parade _____ at four o'clock. Ask: *What is the past tense of* begin? Invite a volunteer to write *began* in the blank. Then read the completed sentence with students. Provide copies of Blackline Master 66 to pairs of students. Read aloud and discuss the directions. Have students complete the page independently and exchange with their partner. Partners check each other's work.

Informal Assessment

Refer students to the chart of verbs on page 254. Assign a verb to each pair of students. Ask them to write a sentence using each tense of the verb. Then invite students to read their sentences aloud to the class.

Use the following chart to assess and reteach.

Are students able to:	
orally explain how irregular verbs change their spelling?	Reteach using the Language Support Activity on TE page 252 and 254.
complete irregular verb charts in three tenses?	Reteach using the Reteach Activity on TE page 253.
Identify the present, present past, and past with *have, has,* or *had* of irregular verbs?	Reteach using the Reteach Activity on TE page 255.

Arrange Irregular Verbs

done	began	ran	run	did
given	grown	began	gave	grew

Present	Past	Past with *have, has,* or *had*
do		
run		
give		
grow		
begin		

Verb Pictures

Look at the pictures and read the verbs in the chart. Cut out the picture that goes in each blank. Paste or glue the pictures in the chart. Write the correct form of the verb under the picture.

Present	Past	Past with *have, has,* or had
_____	ràn	run
Say	Said	_____
eat	_____	eaten
sing	sang	_____

Write Irregular Verbs

Read the paragraph. In each blank, write the form of the verb indicated.

We _____ to my Aunt's house for Thanksgiving.
      (go, past)

After my aunt sliced the turkey, she _____ me some white
               (give, past)

meat—my favorite! I _____ everything on my plate.
      (eat, past)

Later, we _____ songs around the piano.
      (sing, past)

Then my aunt _____ to me, "I think my
        (say, past)

cat _____ away again." I looked everywhere for him.
      (run, past)

I told my aunt I _____ the cat under the table before
      (see, past with have, has, or had)

dinner. I finally found him in the pantry. He _____ the rest
               (eat, past with have, has, or had)

of the turkey!

CONTRACTIONS WITH *NOT*

I. DEVELOP ORAL LANGUAGE
Oral Focus on Grammar Skill

Objective: Explain how verbs with *not* change to contractions

Whole Group Oral Language Activity

Say to students as you demonstrate: *I cannot reach the ceiling.* Have them repeat the sentence aloud. Then tell students that there is a way to say the sentence faster by leaving out some letters. Write *cannot* on the chalkboard. Ask a volunteer to suggest which letters to leave out. Cross out *no.* Then ask students if they know how to show that letters have been left out. Prompt the answer and write an apostrophe above *no.* Write *can't* next to it.

Explain that verbs can make contractions with *not.* Write this list of two words and contractions on the chalkboard: *did not/didn't, were not/weren't, cannot/can't, are not/aren't, was not/wasn't, do not/don't, is not/isn't, has not/hasn't, have not/haven't.* Lead students to recite the list a couple of times as you point to the words.

Scaffolded Verbal Prompting

Use the following verbal prompts to help students better understand.

Nonverbal Prompt for Active Participation

Pre-Production: *Clap when you hear a contraction as I read the list on the chalkboard.*

One- or Two-Word Response Prompt

Early Production: *Say the contraction for* were not. *For* does not. *Tell me what two words make up the contraction* hasn't.

Prompt for Short Answers to Higher-Level Thinking Skills

Speech Emergence: *What two letters are replaced by the apostrophe in the contractions?* (no) *What is the verb in the contraction* don't? (do)

Prompt for Detailed Answers to Higher-Level Thinking Skills

Intermediate and Advanced Fluency: *Explain in a sentence how to change* do not *to a contraction.*

II. DEVELOP GRAMMAR SKILLS IN CONTEXT
Visual/Physical Focus on Grammar Skill

Objective: Develop and demonstrate understanding of contractions with *not*.

Materials: Blackline Master 67; scissors; glue

Whole Group Activity

On the chalkboard write *hadn't, weren't, isn't.* Then write *had not, were not, is not* below in mixed up order. Ask volunteers to come up and write the contractions under the words they go with. Then provide students with copies of Blackline Master 67. Direct students to cut out the contractions at the top of the page. Call out each pair of words in the chart and have students agree on the correct contraction before they paste or glue it in the space below the pair of words. Then have students say the list of paired words and contractions aloud together. If some students come up with the contraction *won't,* use it as an opportunity to teach how *will not* becomes *won't.* Point out that this is different from how other contractions are made. They just have to remember that *won't* is the contraction of *will not.*

Small Group Activity

TPR

Divide students into groups of four. Have each student cut out two contractions at the top of Blackline Master 67. When you call out the pair of words that match that contraction, have the students with that contraction stand up, hop on one foot, and paste the contraction below the pair of words. When you have called all the words, have students in each group help each other to finish their pages.

Partner Activity

Extension: Have each student write a sentence using two contractions in the column he or she first completed. Students check and compare their sentences.

Partners can each take one column on Blackline Master 67 and paste in the correct contractions. Then the student who completed column one asks the other student: *What is the contraction for* is not? Students take turns and continue asking each other until they both have the page completed.

Technology Link

Copy a different set of sentences or a paragraph for each pair of students into a word processing program. Ask students to copy and paste all the contractions with *not* into a list. Then help students create a class list of contractions with *not,* including the two words that make up each contraction.

III. PRACTICE GRAMMAR SKILLS
Written Focus on Grammar Skill

Use the following Blackline Masters to reinforce using contractions with *not* correctly.

Introduce Blackline Master 68: No, They Can't!

Objective: Change a verb and *not* to a contraction

Materials: Blackline Master 68; pen or pencil

[Answers: can't, didn't, isn't, hasn't, doesn't]

Remind students that in a contraction, letters are left out. Ask: *What mark of punctuation shows where the letters are left out?* (apostrophe) Write on the chalkboard: *William did not write the letter.* Underline *did not.* Ask a volunteer to write the sentence again using the contraction. Then distribute Blackline Master 68. Read aloud and discuss the directions with students. Have them complete the page individually.

Informal Assessment

Go around the room round-robin style and give each student either a verb and *not* or a contraction from the chart on page 256. Have students quickly give the other form.

Introduce Blackline Master 69: Fix Contractions with *Not*

Objective: Recognize incorrect contractions with *not* and provide correct ones.

Materials: Blackline Master 69; pen or pencil

[Answers: doesn't, isn't, won't, didn't, can't, didn't, hadn't]

Write a few incorrect subjects and contractions with *not* on the chalkboard, such as *he aren't, I doesn't, they wasn't, Jenny haven't,* and so on. Ask students to read them aloud with you. Then ask a volunteer to provide a correct contraction for each incorrect one. Write them on the chalkboard. Then give each student a copy of Blackline Master 69. Have students work individually to complete the page. Then have partners read each other's corrections. If any are different, encourage students to decide if both answers can be correct.

Informal Assessment

Read sentences from More Practice on page 257. Ask students to tell you the two words for each contraction. Have students write each contraction and the two words in a chart.

Use the following chart to assess and reteach.

Are students able to:	
orally identify contractions with *not?*	Reteach using the Language Support Activity on TE page 256.
change a verb and *not* to a contraction and a contraction to a verb with *not?*	Reteach using the Language Support Activity on TE page 256.
write sentences with contractions with *not?*	Reteach using the Reteach Activity on TE page 257.

Contraction Cut-Outs

hasn't	don't
isn't	can't
aren't	doesn't
wasn't	didn't

is not	does not
was not	are not
did not	can not
has not	do not

No, They Can't!

Read the questions and look at the pictures. Then read the answers. Write the answer again with a contraction for the underlined words.

Can birds drive cars?

No, they <u>cannot</u>. _____

Did the helicopters sing?

No, they <u>did not</u>. _____

Is the dog cooking breakfast?

No, it <u>is not</u>. _____

Has the doctor eaten the palm tree?

No, she <u>has not</u>. _____

Does the telephone do the laundry?

No, it <u>does not</u>. _____

Name_____ Date_____

Fix Contractions with *Not*

Read the sentences. Cross out the incorrect contraction and write a correct one above it.

The computer don't work.

My sister haven't repaired it yet.

Now my paper aren't finished.

My teacher weren't be happy if my assignment is late.

I doesn't get a good grade.

My sister aren't fix the computer until Saturday.

I wasn't meet my friends that day because I have to type my paper.

My dad said he hadn't going to shoot baskets with me until I finish.

I wish I can't agreed to turn in the paper on Monday.

SUFFIXES

Introduce this lesson before Pupil Edition pages 274–275.

I. DEVELOP ORAL LANGUAGE
Oral Focus on Vocabulary Skill

Objective: Identify and use suffixes -er, -or, -less, -able, -ly, and -ful.

Whole Group Oral Language Activity

Write the word *teacher* on the chalkboard. Say: *I am your teacher.* Point to the word *teacher.* Say: *I am also a writer, walker, and biker.* Write each noun on the chalkboard as you say it. Discuss with students what they noticed about each word. Explain that the suffixes -er and -or means *one who,* so a teacher is "one who teaches," and a visitor is "one who visits." Use the same type of process to introduce the other suffixes: -less (without), -able (able to be), -ly (in a ___ way) and -ful (full of).

Scaffolded Verbal Prompting

Use the following verbal prompts to help students better understand words with suffixes.

Nonverbal Prompt for Active Participation

Pre-Production: Write a suffix (-er, -or, -less, -able, -ly, and -ful) on each card and give one card to each student. Say: *Hold up your card only if the word I say contains your suffix.*

TPR
One- or Two-Word Response Prompt

Early Production: *Which word means* able to be used: useful *or* usable? *(usable) What does the other word mean? (full of use)*

Prompt for Short Answers to Higher-Level Thinking Skills

Speech Emergence: *How would you change the word* helpful *to make a word that means* without help?

Prompt for Detailed Answers to Higher-Level Thinking Skills

Intermediate and Advanced Fluency: *Why is it important to pay attention to suffixes when you read, write, or speak?*

II. DEVELOP VOCABULARY SKILLS IN CONTEXT
Visual/Physical Focus on Vocabulary Skill

Objective: Identify words with suffixes -er, -or, -less, -able, -ly, and -ful.

Small Group Activity

Assign one suffix to each group. Have groups brainstorm words for their suffix and record them on paper. Then have members of the group each write one word and its definition on a slip of paper. Have students exchange papers, read their definitions, and have the rest of the group name the word.

Technology Link

Invite students to create a suffix index using word-processing software. Encourage them to add to the list as they discover more words with each suffix.

Partner Activity

Have partners make a set of cards for the suffixes *-er, -or, -less, -able, -ly,* and *-ful.* Give each pair several slips of paper on which you have recorded words for these suffixes. Taking turns, have partners choose a slip of paper, create a word with one of the suffix cards, and then act it out for the other to guess.

III. PRACTICE VOCABULARY SKILLS
Written Focus on Vocabulary Skill

Practice A

Objective: Identify the word with the suffix *-er, -or, -less, -able, -ly,* and *-ful* that matches a definition.

Materials: Blackline Master 70; pencils

[Answers: 1. catcher; 2. scoreless; 3. loudly; 4. successful; 5. likeable; 6. player; 7. spotless; 8. fixable; 9. sweetly; 10. sailor]

Practice B

Objective: Identify words with suffixes *-er, -or, -less, -able, -ly,* and *-ful* and associate them with their meanings.

Materials: Blackline Master 71; pencils

[Answers: 1. reachable; 2. endless; 3. enjoyable; 4. player; 5. willful; 6. easily; 7. sailor; 8. visitor; 9. lifeless; 10. sweetly; 11. joyful; 12. talker]

Introduce Blackline Master 70: Look for Suffixes

Distribute Blackline Master 70. Read the directions with students and work through the first exercise with them. Read the first definition. Ask students which of the answer choices has the suffix that means *one who catches. (catcher)* Tell students to circle that word. Then have them complete the rest of the exercises.

Introduce Blackline Master 71: Suffix Crossword

Distribute Blackline Master 71. Read the directions with students and make sure they understand what they are to do. Work through the first exercise with students. Demonstrate on the chalkboard how to write the answer in the boxes on the puzzle. Then have them complete the rest of the sentences independently. Point out that for clue 6, the *y* changes to an *i* before adding the suffix.

Informal Assessment

Have students turn to page 275 in the textbook. Refer them to exercise one in Practice A. Ask, *What does the suffix* -less *in the word* scoreless *mean? (without)* Next, read aloud exercise 6 in Practice B. Ask, *What is an announcer? (An announcer is a person who announces something.)*

Use the following chart to assess and reteach.

Are students able to:	
change the meaning of words by adding suffixes *-er, -or, -less, -able, -ly,* and *-ful?*	Reteach by using the Language Support Activity on TE page 274.
identify the meanings of words with suffixes *-er, -or, -less, -able, -ly,* and *-ful?*	Reteach by using the Reteach Activity on TE page 275.

Look for Suffixes

Read each definition. Read the words beside each definition. Circle the word that matches each definition.

1. one who catches   catcher   catchable

2. without score   scorable   scoreless

3. in a loud way   loudly   louder

4. full of success   successor   successful

5. able to be liked   likeable   likely

6. one who plays   playful   player

7. without a spot   spotless   spotter

8. able to be fixed   fixable   fixer

9. in a sweet way   sweetest   sweetly

10. one who sails   sailable   sailor

Name_____ Date_____

Suffix Crossword

Read each clue. The underlined word is the base word of the answer. Write in the puzzle the word with a suffix that matches the clue.

Across

1. able to be <u>reach</u>ed

4. one who <u>play</u>s

7. one who <u>sail</u>s

9. without <u>life</u>

10. in a <u>sweet</u> way

11. full of <u>joy</u>

12. one who <u>talk</u>s

Down

2. without <u>end</u>

3. able to be <u>enjoy</u>ed

5. full of <u>will</u>

6. in an <u>easy</u> way

8. one who <u>visit</u>s

WRITING DESCRIPTIONS

Introduce this lesson before Pupil Edition pages 276–277.

I. DEVELOP ORAL LANGUAGE
Oral Focus on Composition Skill

Objective: Use sensory details to orally describe a picture.

Whole Group Oral Language Activity

Have students look at the picture on page 277. Ask them to describe what they see. Prompt them to use sensory words by asking questions such as these: *Are the buildings small or tall? What colors are they? What might you hear as you looked at these buildings? What might you smell?* Write students' responses on the chalkboard, and label each one by the sense to which it appeals.

Scaffolded Verbal Prompting

Use the following verbal prompts to help students describe.

Nonverbal Prompt for Active Participation

Pre-Production: *Show me what you might do if you smelled a skunk.*

One- or Two-Word Response Prompt

Early Production: *If you smelled a skunk, what word might you use to describe it?*

Prompt for Short Answers to Higher-Level Thinking Skills

Speech Emergence: *Tell about something you heard. Use a word that describes the sound.*

Prompt for Detailed Answers to Higher-Level Thinking Skills

Intermediate Fluency: *In a sentence, tell about something you tasted. Use a word to describe the taste.*

II. DEVELOP COMPOSITION SKILLS IN CONTEXT
Visual/Physical Focus on Composition Skill

Objective: Play a guessing game to practice sensory words.

Small Group Activity

Give each group a series of index cards on which you have drawn or pasted pictures of words that can be described by one of the five senses. Under the pictures, write *sight, sound, touch, taste,* or *smell.* Have students take turns finding sensory words that fit each picture. For example, if there is a picture of an apple and the word *taste* is written under it, the answer might be *sweet.*

Technology Link

Have students make more sensory cards on the computer. They can either use clip art and add the sensory word labels, or they can type the sensory words and paste them onto pictures they have drawn or cut from magazines.

Extension: Ask pairs to write a paragraph describing one of the items they have named in the quiz game.

Partner Activity

Have partners quiz each other by doing the following. The first person says the name of an item and one of the five senses. The second person must then think of a sensory word that describes that item. Example: Partner 1: *kitten, touch;* Partner 2: *soft*

III. PRACTICE COMPOSITION SKILLS
Written Focus on Composition Skill

Practice A

Objective: Classify words according to the sense to which they appeal.

Materials: Blackline Master 72; scissors; glue or paste

[**Answers:** Sight: *bright, green;* Sound: *loud, squeaky;* Touch: *hard, rough;* Taste: *sweet, salty* (also, *burnt*); Smell: *stinky, burnt* (also, *sweet, salty*)]

Practice B

Objective: Use words that appeal to the sense indicated.

Materials: Blackline Master 73; pencil

[**Answers:** will vary. Possible responses: 1. little, 2. flat, 3. banging, 4. heavy, 5. squeaky, 6, dark, 7. sweet, 8. loud, 9. dry, 10. happy]

Introduce Blackline Master 72: Which Sense?

Distribute copies of Blackline Master 72. Read the directions aloud with students. Point out that some words can appeal to more than one sense. For example, an apple can *taste* fresh, but it can also *smell* fresh. Tell them to choose either one as they complete Blackline Master 72.

Introduce Blackline Master 73: A Surprise

Make student pairs of varying levels. Have them work together to come up with words to complete the sentences. Distribute Blackline Master 73 to each student. Read the directions, and do the first item with students, proposing several different answers, such as *little, small, big, tall, green,* and so on. Have students complete their papers, then share their answers. Compare the stories that arise from the different sensory words.

Informal Assessment

Have students turn to page 193 in their textbooks and look at the picture at the bottom of the page. Ask them to give two sensory words to describe what they see in the picture.

Use the following chart to assess and reteach.

Are students able to: identify and classify sensory words?	Reteach by allowing pre- and early production students to pantomime or draw their responses.
use sensory words to describe?	Reteach by using the Reteach Activity on TE page 277.

Name_____ Date_____

Which Sense?

Look at the sense word in each box. Cut out the words in the right column.
Glue these words into the box with the name of the sense they describe.
(Some of them could fit in more than one box.)

Sight
Sound
Touch
Taste
Smell

stinky

sweet

hard

bright

rough

salty

loud

green

squeaky

burnt

A Surprise

Read each sentence. On the line, write a word that describes by telling about one of the senses. The word should be about the sense in ( ).

1. Maya lived in a _____ house. (sight)

2. The roof was very _____. (sight)

3. One day, she came home and heard a _____ noise. (sound)

4. She pushed against the _____ front door. (touch)

5. The _____ hinges made a noise. (sound)

6. Maya walked toward the _____ kitchen. (sight)

7. What was that? It was a _____ smell. (smell)

8. She heard a _____ noise on the roof. (sound)

9. She went up the stairs, scared. Her mouth tasted

   _____. (taste)

10. "Surprise! Happy birthday, Maya," everyone shouted in

    _____ voices. (sound)

WRITING THAT COMPARES

Introduce this lesson before Pupil Edition pages 286–301.

I. PREWRITE
Oral Warm Up

Objectives:
- Use visual reasoning to compare.
- Relate observations.

TPR

Whole Group Oral Language Activity

Hold up two identical pencils and ask students if they are alike or different. Then hold up one of the pencils and a crayon and ask: *Are these two things alike? How are they different?*

Review that when students compare two things, they say how they are alike, same, or different. Ask a volunteer for words that show how the pencil and crayon are the same. Ask students to think of words that tell how they are different. Then have them brainstorm how the following are alike and different and write their responses in charts on the board: a lake and a swimming pool, a cat and a dog, a mango and a banana.

Objectives:
- Use a graphic organizer to compare.
- Practice comparative writing

Materials: Blackline Master 74; pencils

Introduce the Writing Mode

Explain that students can use comparisons in their writing to explain how things are alike and different. Model comparative writing. *(Example: You can swim in both a lake and a swimming pool. Lakes are always outside. Pools can be indoors. Lake water is fresh water from a stream. Pool water is pumped into the pool and treated with chemicals to keep it fresh.)*

Pre-Production and Early Production

Scaffolded Writing Instruction

Using Blackline Master 74, have students choose two items to compare and draw a picture of them at the top. Then have them draw details from their pictures that focus on an attribute that is the same or different in each row of boxes. Have them circle "Same" or "Different" as fits that detail.

Speech Emergence

Have students choose two items to compare and label each picture with words or phrases. Also have them circle the word "Same" or "Different."

Intermediate and Advanced Fluency

Have students choose two items to compare, draw them in the top row and then create a sentence. Have them circle "Same" and "Different" and write sentences in the boxes that compare or contrast. They may illustrate their sentences if they wish.

Research and Inquiry: Search Online

Guide students through the process of an online search by showing them how to find a search engine, type in a keyword and click on *search,* and select suggested sites. Suggest ways that students can narrow their topics and use more precise keywords. Model this process by conducing a sample keyword search on a favorite search engine.

II. DRAFT

Focus on Writing That Compares

Objectives:
• Organize details that compare and contrast.
• Begin drafting comparative writing.

Blackline Master 75—
Compare Two Things

Ask students what is confusing about this comparison: *A crayon makes colored marks, but a pencil has an eraser. (The characteristics being compared are different.)* Then model how to present details in an order that makes sense: *A pencil and a crayon are alike in some ways. We can use both of them to draw or write. A pencil and a crayon are also different. A pencil makes gray marks and a crayon makes colored marks. A pencil has an eraser, but a crayon does not.*

Ask students to tell what they are going to write about, and have the class brainstorm details about their topics.

If Speech Emergence or Intermediate and Advanced Fluency students wish to write about a different subject than the one they chose for Blackline Master 74, tell them to make a new chart before they begin writing.

Scaffolded Writing Instruction

Pre-Production & Early Production

Blackline Master 75—
Compare Two Things

Use Blackline Master 75 to help students organize and add details to their comparisons. Have students draw pictures to show the two things being compared at the top of the page. Have them draw one picture to show how the two subjects are both alike in the second section. Have them draw another picture to show how the two things are different in the third and fourth sections.

Speech Emergence

Blackline Master 76—
Compare Two Things

Use Blackline Master 76 to guide students in their comparative writing. Have them draw and write words or short phrases to compare and contrast.

Intermediate and Advanced Fluency

Students may begin to write their comparisons. Encourage them to explain how two things are alike, explain how two things are different, and to organize their details in an order that makes sense. Guide them to use comparing and contrasting words to connect ideas.

III. REVISE

Focus on Elaboration

Objectives:
- Revise writing that compares.
- Add compare/ contrast words and details.

Write the following sentences on the board and read them aloud with the class: *Dogs and cats are both good family pets. In some ways they are alike. People have to feed them and make sure they are healthy. They are also different. Dogs have to go outside to get exercise, but cats can stay inside.*

Ask volunteers to circle words that show comparison. Then list other compare/contrast words on the board and encourage students to use them in their writing, such as: *alike, same, like, another, too, unlike, in another way.* Ask volunteers to add other comparisons to the ones on the board to make the comparisons more specific.

Scaffolded Instruction for Revising

Pre-Production & Early Production

Have students choose one or two words from the list and add these details to their drawings. Have them label the new details.

Speech Emergence

Use students' work on Blackline Master 76 to help them organize their comparisons by adding details and revising order. Have them add pictures that provide more details.

Intermediate and Advanced Fluency

Students may elaborate by adding details that point out differences and similarities and using comparing and contrasting words to connect ideas.

Technology Link

Have partners use the thesaurus in the Tools menu to look for synonyms for comparing and contrasting words, and to find a synonym for a word that they repeat often in their writing.

IV. REVISE • PEER CONFERENCING

Focus on Peer Conferencing

Objectives:
- Participate in peer conferences.
- Give and receive suggestions for improvement.
- Revise writing that compares.

Pair emerging speakers and ask them to read each others' writing and describe the pictures. Have more fluent speakers assist pre-and early production students to find or act out words that express their ideas. Have more fluent speakers point to each word as they read their writing and encourage pre-production students to ask questions.

Use page 295 as a guide and write a checklist for each language proficiency level on the chalkboard. Readers can refer to them as they hold their peer-conferences.

V. PROOFREAD

Objectives:
• Use main and helping verbs
• Practice proofreading strategies

Materials: Blackline Master 77; pencils

[Answers: for Blackline Master 77: **A.** all: first word is helping verb; second word is main verb **B.** 1. can drink 2. were flying 3. will sleep 4. found 5. had run]

Spelling Tip:
Invite students to add words from the board to their word cards. Encourage them to arrange their cards in alphabetical order.

Focus on English Conventions

Say and write the following sentences. Underline the main and helping verbs: *We will visit a museum this week. We have bought tickets to a movie. The movie was filmed in South Africa.*

Explain that a main verb shows what the subject is or does. A helping verb helps the main verb to show when the action occurs. Ask students to circle the helping verb in each sentence. List helping verbs on the chalkboard and ask volunteers to say a sentence or a phrase that includes a helping verb and a main verb.

Have students complete Blackline Master 77 to practice the grammar skill before rereading their work to look for main verbs that may be missing a helping verb. Explain that proofreading includes checking for spelling mistakes. Have students make sure that the two items they compare are spelled correctly. Have them use a dictionary to check their spelling.

Model using a dictionary with a student who requests spelling help. After locating the word, show how to read the word entry to find how the plural of the word is formed (if it is a noun) or how the word endings are formed (if it is a verb). Display the word entry to the class.

VI. PUBLISH

Objectives:
• Present a neat final copy of comparative writing.
• Actively view the work of others.

TRP

Use page 298 as a guide and write and read aloud a checklist for each language proficiency level. Encourage students to use the checklist as they prepare a final draft.

Create a Bulletin Board Display

Place students in groups of varying language abilities to share their work. Suggest that students find pictures that they can use for a bulletin board display of their work. Encourage students to use a large flat surface, such as the floor, to arrange their work. Suggest that they could arrange their work by subject matter.

VII. LISTENING, SPEAKING, VIEWING, REPRESENTING

Adapt the steps on pages 298–299 to create activities that will bring out the talents of all students. Encourage pre- and early production students to use peer-translators or helpers, or to act out their ideas.

Informal Assessment

TPR

When assessing students' learning, you will need to adapt your expectations of what constitutes an appropriate response. For example, you may wish to have students act out or draw a response to a verbal or written prompt rather than give a traditional answer.

Name_____ Date_____

Same or Different?

Think about two things you can compare. Draw the two things. Then draw or write to show three ways they are the same or different. Finally, circle *Same* or *Different*.

Compare

Same or Different

Same or Different

Same or Different

Name_____ Date_____

Compare Two Things

Draw the two things you will compare. Draw pictures to show a way the two things are the same. Then draw pictures to show ways the two things are different.

1.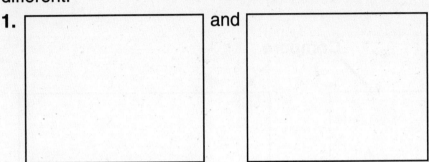

and

are the same and different

2. They both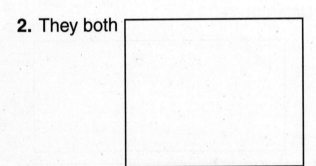

3.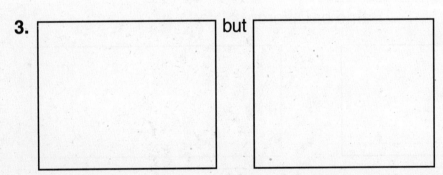

but

4.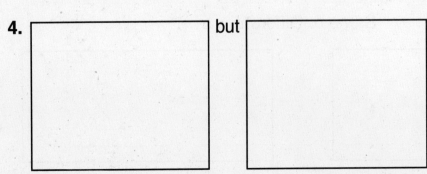

but

Name_____ Date_____

Comparing Two Things

Draw or write the two things you will compare. Tell how the two things are alike. Tell how the two things are different. Then use words, phrases, and sentences to compare. Finally, draw detailed pictures.

How I Compare [ ] **and** [ ]

1. (Alike) Both

2. (Difference)

3. (Difference)

Main and Helping Verbs

A. Draw one line under the main verb. Draw two lines under the helping verb.

1. shall come

2. had trained

3. have studied

4. was barking

5. could meet

6. will fly

7. can run

8. is crawling

B. Complete each sentence. Choose the correct verb or main and helping verb.

1. An elephant _____ with its trunk. _____

   can drink   drink

2. The birds _____ overhead this morning. _____

   flying   were flying

3. The bears _____ all this winter. _____

   will sleep   is sleep

4. Yesterday, the raccoon _____ our garbage. _____

   found   can found

5. The cheetah was tired because it _____ all day._____

   run   had run

SUBJECT AND OBJECT PRONOUNS

I. DEVELOP ORAL LANGUAGE
Oral Focus on Grammar Skill

Objective: Orally identify pronouns and tell whether they replace a subject or an object.

Whole Group Oral Language Activity

Invite students to look at the photograph on student textbook page 324. Point to the girl with the camera. Ask: *Who is taking a picture?* Write student responses, such as *The girl is taking a picture.* Show another way of writing this sentence. *She is taking a picture.* Point out how the noun girl is replaced with the pronoun *she.* Explain that a pronoun is a word that can take the place of one or more nouns. Also point out that a pronoun must agree with the noun it replaces. List the singular and plural pronouns separately on the chalkboard.

Remind students that a pronoun, just like a noun, can be the subject of a sentence or the object of a verb. Explain that when a noun is the subject of the sentence, the pronoun that replaces it should be a subject pronoun. That is why the pronoun *she* was used the replace the noun *girl* in the sentence: *She is taking a picture.*

Look at the same photo and remind students that the object is the person or thing that the action of the sentence is done to. Point to the original sentence on the chalkboard. Ask: *What is the girl taking?* Write student responses: *a picture.* The object of this sentence is *picture.* Ask a volunteer to tell what object pronoun could replace *picture* in this sentence. *(it)* Write: *The girl is taking it.* Have them read the sentence aloud. Read aloud the object pronoun for each subject pronoun listed on the chalkboard.

Scaffolded Verbal Prompting

Use the following verbal prompts to help students better understand subject and object pronouns.

Nonverbal Prompt for Active Participation

Pre-production: *Look at the picture on page 324. Point to one of the people. Show me what she is doing.*

One- or Two-Word Response Prompt

Early Production: *Point to a person in the picture. Which word would you use to name each person?*

Prompt for Short Answers to Higher-Level Thinking Skills

Speech Emergence: *Tell who is in the picture. Tell what each person is doing. Use a pronoun to name that person.*

Prompt for Detailed Answers to Higher-Level Thinking Skills

Intermediate and Advanced Fluency: *Tell me, in one sentence, who is in the picture and what she is doing. Repeat the sentence. Replace the subject with a pronoun. Replace the object with a pronoun.*

II. DEVELOP GRAMMAR SKILLS IN CONTEXT
Visual/Physical Focus on Grammar Skill

Objective: Develop and demonstrate an understanding of subject and object pronouns.

Blackline Master 78

TPR

Extension: Continue the above activity with these sentences: *Ann and Mia went to the store. Jim and Terrence went with them. I saw Mike and Rosa. Mike and Rosa were talking to Sam and Dave.* Point out that students are using the plural subject and object pronouns *they* and *them.*

Extension: Have students make example sentences to accompany their charts.

Whole Group Activity

Provide each student with a copy of Blackline Master 78. Tell them to color the *she* card red, the *her* card pink, the *he* card blue, and the *him* card green. Have students cut out each card.

Write several sentences on the chalkboard with the names of boys as subject in some and object in others, and with the names of girls as subject in some and object in others. For example: *Ray visited Kelly. Maria saw Anthony. Lisa called Todd. Anna met Melinda.*

Ask students to hold up the correct card to replace each of the subject words and each of the object words as you read them aloud.

Small Group Activity

Ask each student to write two sentences with the name of a person as the subject of each. Then have each student pass his or her sentence to the student to his/her right. That student must replace the name with the correct pronoun, either *he* or *she.*

Do the same thing with object nouns and pronouns.

Partner Activity

Have partners work together to make a "Subject-Object Pronouns" chart. Tell them to make three columns, with the headings "Subject" and "Object" on the second and third columns. Then have them write "Singular" on the next line of the first column, and "Plural" on the next line of the first column. Ask students to fill in the subject and object pronouns they know and use it as they write.

Technology Link

Have pairs of students make their charts on the computer, using a table format and printing it out.

III. PRACTICE GRAMMAR SKILLS
Written Focus on Grammar Skills

Use Blackline Masters 79 and 80 to reinforce using pronouns correctly.

Introduce Blackline Master 79: Place the Pronouns

Objective: Replace nouns with the correct pronouns.

Materials: Blackline Master 79; scissors; paste or glue

[**Answers:** 1. her, 2. They, 3. We, 4. us, 5. them, 6. She, 7. He, 8. Him]

Distribute Blackline Master 79. Have students cut out the pronoun cards along the dotted lines. Read aloud and discuss the instructions with students. Model placing the pronoun in the first sentence. Ask: *What word would you use to replace the word in parentheses? (her)* Encourage students to work in pairs of varying reading levels, and have them work together to make the sentences.

Informal Assessment

Have students turn to the picture on textbook page 326. Say this sentence: *The girl is holding a dog.* Ask students what pronoun they would use to replace *The girl* in that sentence. *(She)*

Introduce Blackline Master 80: Which Word?

Objective: Choose the correct pronoun to complete each sentence.

Materials: Blackline Master 80

[**Answers:** 1. It, 2. her, 3. them, 4. He, 5. it, 6. us]

Distribute Blackline Master 80. Tell students they will be choosing a subject or object pronoun to complete the sentences. Ask students to think of which word makes sense in each sentence. Is it about a thing? Then you would not use a pronoun for a person, such as *he* or *she.* Is it about more than one person? Then you would use a plural pronoun. Is it the subject of the sentence? Then you would use a subject pronoun? Is it the object? Then you would use an object pronoun.

Informal Assessment

Point to the picture on page 327. Say this sentence: *The cars drive along the road.* Ask students which pronoun they might use to replace *cars.(They)*

Use the following chart to assess and reteach:

Are students able to:	
orally replace nouns with pronouns?	Reteach using the Language Support activity on TE page 324.
decide which pronoun completes a sentence?	Reteach using the Language Support activity on TE page 324.
identify which pronouns replace subjects and which replace objects?	Reteach using the Reteach Activities on TE page 325 and 327.

she

her

he

him

Name_____ Date_____

Place the Pronouns

Cut out the pronoun cards. Read each sentence. Paste one of the cards in the blank to replace the word in ( ).

she	he	him	her
they	them	we	us

1. Lee saw (Alice) ⬚ today.

2. (Lee and Alice) ⬚ are doing a project together.

3. (Sam and I) ⬚ want to help them.

4. Will they let (Sam and I) ⬚ help?

5. I want to ask (Lee and Alice) ⬚.

6. (Alice) ⬚ said it was OK with her.

7. (Sam) ⬚ will ask Lee.

8. Then I will tell (Rob). ⬚

Which Word?

Read each sentence. Think about which word in ( ) best completes the sentence. Circle that word.

1. The car is old. (It, He) breaks a lot.

2. When did you see (she, her)?

3. I asked (them, they) a question.

4. Lana wrote to Jim. (Him, He) wrote back.

5. Give me the book. Give (him, it) to me!

6. Uncle Pete gave it to (we, us).

I. DEVELOP ORAL LANGUAGE
Oral Focus on Grammar Skill

Objective: Orally describe pictures, demonstrating pronoun-verb agreement.

Whole Group Oral Language Activity

Ask students to look at the photograph on textbook page 332. Ask a volunteer to describe what is happening in the picture. Write responses on the chalkboard, and begin forming them into sentences beginning with *The girl.* Ask: *What does the girl do? (rides)*

Then ask students to substitute the correct subject pronoun for *The girl. (She)* Write *She rides.* on the chalkboard.

Tell students the rules for pronoun-verb agreement. Explain that just as the verb has to agree with a noun that is the subject of a sentence, the same is true if a pronoun is the subject of a sentence. Point out both sentences on the chalkboard. Change the noun/pronoun to *The girls/They* and ask how each of these changes would affect the verb. *(The letter -s would not be added to ride.)* Write *The girls ride.* and *They ride.* on the chalkboard.

Scaffolded Verbal Prompting

Use the following verbal prompts to help students better understand pronoun-verb agreement.

Nonverbal Prompt for Active Participation

Pre-Production: *Look at the picture on page 333. Point to who is doing the action.*

One- or Two-Word Response Prompt

Early Production: *Name the people in the picture. Tell what they do.*

Prompt for Short Answers to Higher-Level Thinking Skills

Speech Emergence: *Tell who is in the picture. Change that word to a pronoun. Tell what they are doing.*

Prompt for Detailed Answers to Higher-Level Thinking Skills

Intermediate and Advanced Fluency: *Tell what is happening in the picture in one sentence. Use a pronoun instead of a noun to name the subject.*

II. DEVELOP GRAMMAR SKILLS IN CONTEXT
Visual/Physical Focus on Grammar Skill

Objective: Develop and demonstrate understanding of pronoun-verb agreement

Blackline Master 81

[Answers: 1. sings, 2. write, 3. sing, 4. sings, 5. writes, sings]

TPR

Extension: Have students write their stories on the chalkboard. Then have them challenge another group to replace any subject nouns with subject pronouns.

Extension: Have partners share their sentences with another pair of partners. Have each pair check the other's work for correctness.

Whole Group Activity

Distribute copies of Blackline Master 81 to each student. Have them color the *sing* rectangle yellow, the *sings* rectangle green, the *write* rectangle red, and the *writes* rectangle blue. Write the following sentences on the chalkboard and read them aloud. Have students hold up the rectangle with the word that best completes the sentence as you read each one aloud.

1. Marcy (sing, sings) a song.

2. Kara and Abe (write, writes) a story.

3. They (sing, sings) in the chorus, too.

4. Abe (sing, sings) very well.

5. Kara (write, writes) better than she (sing, sings).

Small Group Activity

Give students a list of verbs such as the following: *play, jump, run, skate, swim, go.* Write them on the chalkboard. Ask students to use the verbs to make up stories orally. Tell them to use both nouns and pronouns as the subjects of their sentences. Remind them to make the subjects and verbs agree. Ask for volunteers to share their stories with the class.

Partner Activity

Have one partner come up with a list of five subject pronouns. Have the other partner come up with five verbs. Working together, have the partners construct sentences with those subjects and verbs. Remind them that the subject pronouns and verbs need to agree.

Technology Link

Type a list of subject pronouns and a list of verbs with both singular and plural forms into a word processing program. Pair students of various language levels. Have students use the computer to type complete sentences including the pronouns and the correct form of the verbs. Have them print out their sentences and read them aloud.

III. PRACTICE GRAMMAR SKILLS
Written Focus on Grammar Skills

Use Blackline Masters 82 and 83 to reinforce pronoun-verb agreement.

Introduce Blackline Master 82: A Good Fit

Objective: Choose the correct form of a verb to agree with a subject pronoun.

Materials: Blackline Master 82; scissors; glue or paste

[**Answers:** 1. ties, 2. ride, 3. paint, 4. fits, 5. paints]

Distribute copies of Blackline Master 82 to students. Have them cut out the individual word cards along the dotted lines. Then read the directions aloud with students and discuss them. Have students choose the verb that correctly completes each sentence and paste the word card for that verb in the box. Have pairs of students compare their completed choices.

Informal Assessment

Have students turn to page 336 in their textbooks. Ask them to name the subject pronoun they would use to tell about the two kittens. *(they)*

Have them then make up a sentence using that subject pronoun with a verb that agrees.

Introduce Blackline Master 83: Which Verb?

Objective: Choose the correct verb to agree with a subject pronoun.

Materials: Blackline Master 83

[**Answers:** 1. get, 2. puts, 3. fall, 4. like, 5. make]

Distribute Blackline Master 83 to each student. Read aloud the directions with students and discuss them. Have students work in pairs to discuss the correct answers and circle them on their papers. Ask for volunteers to read their completed sentences aloud.

Informal Assessment

Have students turn to page 337 in their textbooks. Ask what subject pronoun they would use to describe the kitten on that page. *(He or she).* Ask them to make up a sentence about the kitten with a verb that agrees with that pronoun.

Use the following chart to assess and reteach:

Are students able to: orally tell which present-tense verb agrees with a pronoun?	Reteach using the Language Support activity on TE page 332.
identify subject pronouns?	Reteach using the Reteach Activity on TE page 333.
pair subject pronouns correctly with verbs that agree with them?	Reteach using the Rules box on page 332.

sing

sings

write

writes

A Good Fit

Cut out each of the words along the dotted lines. Read the sentences. Decide which word in ( ) best completes the sentence. Paste that word in the box.

tie	ties	ride	rides
paint	paints	fit	fits

1. She (tie, ties) ⬜ her shoes.

2. I (ride, rides) ⬜ my new bike.

3. They (paint, paints) ⬜ the wall.

4. It (fit, fits) ⬜ my sister.

5. He (paint, paints) ⬜ our faces.

Which Verb?

Read each sentence. Decide which verb in ( ) best completes the sentence. Circle that verb.

1. We (get, gets) our toys out.

2. She (put, puts) them in the sand box.

3. They (fall, falls) down.

4. I (like, likes) to play in the sand.

5. You (make, makes) good sand castles.

I. DEVELOP ORAL LANGUAGE
Oral Focus on Grammar Skill

Objective: Orally describe pictures that show possession.

Whole Group Oral Language Activity

Ask students to look at the photo of the bears on page 335. Ask them to point to something on the bears' bodies, such as *the bears' ears.* Ask: *Who do the ears belong to? (the bears)* Write on the chalkboard *the bears' ears,* and point out that the word *bears'* is a possessive noun (a plural one). Tell students that there are pronouns that stand for possessive nouns, and that another way of saying the *bears' ears* would be *their ears.*

Tell students that they can use these possessive pronouns before nouns to show that something belongs to the person or thing: *my, your, his, her, its, our, their.* Explain that there are also possessive pronouns that can be used alone: *mine, yours, his, hers, its, ours, theirs.* Write these sentences as an example:

That hat is Lin's.

That hat is hers.

Scaffolded Verbal Prompting
Use the following verbal prompts to help students better understand possessive pronouns.

Nonverbal Prompt for Active Participation

Pre-Production: *Pick up something in your hand that belongs to you.* Say, for example: *That pencil is Tali's. That is her pencil. That pencil is hers.*

One- or Two-Word Response Prompt

Early Production: Point to objects belonging to various students. Ask: *Whose is that [name of item]?*

Prompt for Short Answers to Higher-Level Thinking Skills

Speech Emergence: Repeat pointing to various objects and asking *Whose is that [name of item]?* Then ask students to replace the name of the person with the correct possessive pronoun.

Prompt for Detailed Answers to Higher-Level Thinking Skills

Intermediate and Advanced Fluency: *Tell me in one sentence about something that belongs to you. Use a possessive pronoun. Then tell me about something that belongs to the student next to you. Use a possessive pronoun.*

II. DEVELOP GRAMMAR SKILLS IN CONTEXT
Visual/Physical Focus on Grammar Skill

Objective: Develop and demonstrate understanding of the use of possessive pronouns.

Blackline Master 84

TPR

Extension: Have children continue the activity making sentences using either *your, his,* or *her* as they refer to other students in the circle.

Extension: Have students make up sentences that show ownership using either *his, hers, its, yours,* or *theirs.*

Whole Group Activity

Distribute a copy of Blackline Master 84 to each child. With students, read aloud the names of the colors printed under each circle. Have students color the circles these colors, then cut out the circles.

Continue pointing out things in the classroom and the people who have or own them: *Malik's hat, Kim's desk, Joe and Lee's poster,* and so on. As you say each one, ask students to hold up the circle with the possessive pronoun that could replace the noun in that phrase. For the above examples, they would hold up *his, her, their.*

Small Group Activity

Have group members sit in a circle. Indicate something of yours and say, *This is Ms. X's pen,* (referring to yourself). Then say *This is my pen.* Have students take turns making sentences in the same way with something of theirs, first naming themselves, then using a possessive pronoun to indicate themselves.

Partner Activity

Have students make up pairs of sentences using the possessive pronouns *mine* and *yours.* Have students refer to each other as they do so.

Technology Link

Have students create a chart of possessive pronouns on the computer. They can divide it into singular and plural, and into possessives that precede a noun and those that stand alone.

III. PRACTICE GRAMMAR SKILLS
Written Focus on Grammar Skills

Use Blackline Masters 85 and 86 to reinforce using possessive nouns correctly.

Introduce Blackline Master 85: Cut and Paste

Objective: Replace possessive nouns with possessive pronouns.

Materials: Blackline Master 85; scissors; glue or paste

[**Answers:** 1. her, 2. Its, 3. Their, 4. hers, 5. mine]

Distribute a copy of Blackline Master 85 to each student. Read aloud the directions, making sure students understand that they will be cutting out possessive pronouns and pasting them over possessive nouns. Have students work in pairs of varying levels and share their completed computer screens with the rest of the group.

Informal Assessment

Ask students to turn to textbook page 340. Ask them to say a sentence that tells about what the boy on the left is carrying, such as, *It is the boy's skateboard.* Then have them replace the possessive noun with a possessive pronoun. *(his)*

Introduce Blackline Master 86: My or Mine?

Objective: Choose the correct form of possessive pronoun, the kind that precedes a noun or the kind that stands alone.

Materials: Blackline Master 86

[**Answers:** 1. Her, 2. Mine, 3. our, 4. their, 5. yours, 6. his, 7. ours, 8. my]

Distribute copies of Blackline Master 86 to all students. Read the directions aloud with students, and complete the first item together as a group.

Informal Assessment

Have children turn to textbook page 338 and look at the picture of the elephant. Say: *The elephant has the elephant's trunk raised.* Ask students to replace the word *elephant's* with the correct possessive pronoun. *(its; his or her would also be acceptable.)*

Use the following chart to assess and reteach:

Are students able to:	
orally identify possessive pronouns?	Reteach using the Reteach Activity on TE page 335.
choose the correct possessive pronoun to replace a possessive noun?	Reteach using the Language Support Activity on TE page 334.
choose the correct possessive pronoun to stand alone or precede a noun?	Reteach using the Guided Practice on page 334, simplifying the sentences as needed.

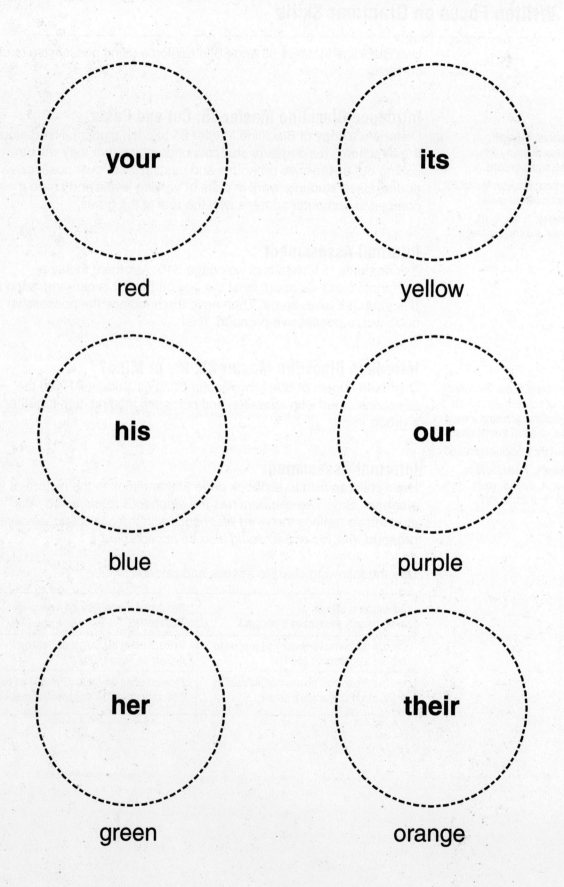

your

its

red

yellow

his

our

blue

purple

her

their

green

orange

Cut and Paste

Cut out the possessive pronouns below along the dotted lines. Look at the computer screen. Paste the pronoun that could take the place of each box on the computer screen.

| hers | Their | Its | mine | her |

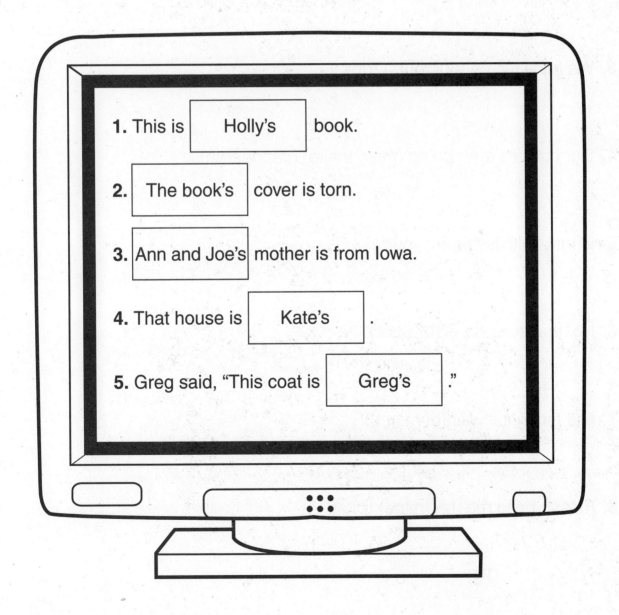

1. This is [Holly's] book.

2. [The book's] cover is torn.

3. [Ann and Joe's] mother is from Iowa.

4. That house is [Kate's].

5. Greg said, "This coat is [Greg's]."

My or Mine?

Read each sentence. Circle the pronoun in ( ) that best completes it.

1. (Her, Hers) favorite place is the zoo.

2. (My, Mine) is the pool.

3. We have fun on (our, ours) trip

4. Our cousins are visiting (their, theirs) grandparents.

5. Is that suitcase (your, yours)?

6. No, that suitcase is (his, her).

7. Mia thought it was (our, ours)!

8. Please bring me (my, mine) ticket.

HOMOPHONES

Introduce this lesson before Pupil Edition pages 352–353.

I. DEVELOP ORAL LANGUAGE
Oral Focus on Vocabulary Skill

Objective: Identify, generate, and use homophones.

Whole Group Oral Language Activity

Write *blue* and *blew* on the chalkboard. Ask a volunteer to read the two words. Show a blue crayon. Point to *blue* and explain that this spelling means the color blue. Have student discuss what the meaning of the word *blew* is. Have a volunteer mime blowing a candle and then use *blew* in a sentence to say what he/she did. Explain that in the English language some words sound the same but have different spellings. These words are homophones.

Follow the same process for other homophone pairs, such as *bee/be, sun/son, read/rode, nose/knows, horse/hoarse,* and *flower/flour.*

Scaffolded Verbal Prompting

Use the following verbal prompts to help children better understand homophones.

Nonverbal Prompt for Active Participation

TPR

One- or Two-Word Response prompt

Prompt for Short Answers to Higher-Level thinking Skills

Prompt for Detailed Answers to Higher-Level thinking Skills

Pre-Production: Write the word *hi.* Say: *This word is* hi *which is what we say when we greet someone. Wave hi to the person standing beside you.* Write the word *high.* Say: *This word is also* high *but it means tall. Now jump as high as you can.* Repeat with other homophone pairs.

Early Production: Write the words *sun* and *son* on the chalkboard. Say: *Spell the word that names a bright object in the sky. (s-u-n)*

Speech Emergence: Write the words *nose* and *knows* on the chalkboard. Say: *Point to one of these words and use it in a sentence that shows you know what the word means.*

Intermediate and Advanced Fluency: Write *right* and *write* on the chalkboard. Ask: *What is the difference between these two words?*

II. DEVELOP VOCABULARY SKILLS IN CONTEXT
Visual/Physical Focus on Vocabulary Skill

Objective: Match homophones to their meanings.

Small Group Activity

Give each group a section of mural paper to work on. Tell students that in their section they are to draw a picture of a zoo, a park, a forest, or some other place where animals live. In the mural, they should include five pictures of words that are homophones. Have students write on a separate sheet of paper a list of the homophones they used. Beside each homophone, have them write the other spelling of the word. Post each list beside its mural and have other students find those homophones in the picture.

Partner Activity

Have partners make flashcards for difficult homophone pairs. Have students write each word on a separate index card and either draw a picture or write a definition on the back of the card. Then have partners draw cards from each other and use that word correctly in a sentence.

Technology Link

Show students how to create flash cards by making two-column tables in a word-processing program. Have students write a homophone in the left column and its meaning in the right column. Have students print out their tables, cut each row and fold the meaning behind the word as they practice each word.

III. PRACTICE VOCABULARY SKILLS
Written Focus on Vocabulary Skill

Practice A

Objective: Identify the homophone that matches a picture

Materials: Blackline Master 87; pencils

[**Answers:** 1. bee; 2. nose; 3. horse; 4. road; 5. son; 6. pair; 7. sum; 8. tail; 9. plane]

Practice B

Objective: Use homophones correctly in sentences

Materials: Blackline Master 88; pencils, crayons or markers

[**Answers:** Check students' drawings and labels.
1. week, weak; 2. deer, dear; 3. nose, knows; 4. ate, eight]

Introduce Blackline Master 87: Find the Homophones

Distribute Blackline Master 87. Read the directions with children and complete the first example with them. Discuss the meaning of the homophones below the picture of each word. Ask students to circle the word that names the insect *bee*. Check children's work. Then have them complete the rest of the exercises.

Introduce Blackline Master 88: Choose the Homophone

Distribute Blackline Master 88. Complete the first exercise with children. Read the first two sentences. Discuss the meaning of each homophone. Then ask a volunteer to reread the first sentence. Discuss which homophone belongs in that sentence. Have students write the word on the line. Check children's work. Then have them complete the rest of the puzzle independently.

Informal Assessment

Have children turn to page 353 in the textbook. Refer them to exercise one in Practice A. Ask, *What do the homophones* k-n-o-w-s *and* n-o-s-e *mean?* (K-n-o-w-s *means that you know or understand something. Your n-o-s-e is on your face and you use it to smell with.*) Refer them to exercise 6 in Practice B. Ask, *What does the word* w-o-n *mean?* (*It means that you beat someone in a race or game. Possible sentence: I was fastest so I won the race.*)

Use the following chart to assess and reteach.

Are students able to: spell homophones and use them in sentences?	Reteach by using the Language Support Activity on TE page 352.
associate the meaning of a homophone with its spelling?	Reteach by using the Reteach Activity on TE page 353.

Name_____ Date_____

Find the Homophone

Look at each picture. Read the homophone pair below each picture. Circle the homophone that matches each picture.

1.

be   bee

2.

nose   knows

3.

horse   hoarse

4.

road   rode

5.

sun   son

6.

pear   pair

7.

some   sum

8.

tale   tail

9.

plane   plain

Choose the Homophone

Read each sentence. Read the homophones below the sentences. Write the correct homophone on the lines. Draw a picture to show one of the homophones. Label your picture with its homophone.

1. Last _____ I went to the zoo.

The sick lion looked _____.

week   weak

2. Some _____ licked salt off my hand.

My _____ pal Tom was scared.

dear   deer

3. An elephant stuck its _____ out.

Tom _____ it is called a trunk.

nose   knows

4. We _____ popcorn and had fun.

We went home at _____ o'clock.

ate   eight

OUTLINE

Introduce this lesson before Pupil Edition pages 354–355.

I. DEVELOP ORAL LANGUAGE
Oral Focus on Composition Skill

Objective: Orally describe a picture and determine the main idea and at least one detail.

Whole Group Oral Language Activity

Direct students' attention to the photograph of the bird on page 355. Ask students what they see in the photo. Tell them that *Birds* might be the topic of what they see. Ask them to come up with a main idea sentence that tells something about birds. Lead them to something like *There are many kinds of birds.* Write it on the chalkboard. Then ask them to look at the picture and think of a detail it shows about the bird. An example might be that the bird has a round shape, its color, that it has a small head, or that it has a tiny beak.

Scaffolded Verbal Prompting

Use the following verbal prompts to help students determine the main idea and details that could be used for an outline.

Nonverbal Prompt for Active Participation

Pre-Production: *Show me something that the bird might do.*

One- or Two-Word Response Prompt

Early Production: *Tell me a word that describes the bird.*

Prompt for Short Answers to Higher-Level Thinking Skills

Speech Emergence: *What would you like to learn about the bird?*

Prompt for Detailed Answers to Higher-Level Thinking Skills

Intermediate Fluency: *In one sentence, tell me a detail about the bird in the picture.*

II. DEVELOP COMPOSITION SKILLS IN CONTEXT
Visual/Physical Focus on Composition Skill

Objective: Come up with a main idea sentence for an outline on a particular topic.

TPR

Small Group Activity

Make a series of index cards with the name of one topic on each. Examples might include a kind of animal, a place, a scientific fact, a historical event, and so on. Shuffle the cards deal them out to each member of the group. The student who gets each card must think of a main idea sentence for that topic and tell it to or act it out for the group.

Technology Link

Have students type their main idea sentences into a word processing program. Allow other students time to add detail sentences to each.

Partner Activity

Extension: Make a round-robin game where students complete a card and pass it to the next student, who adds another detail.

Have each partner make five cards with a main idea sentence about a particular topic. Ask partners to trade cards. Each partner must then write a detail that could come under that main idea sentence in an outline on the partner's card.

III. PRACTICE COMPOSITION SKILLS
Written Focus on Composition Skill

Introduce Blackline Master 89: Big Cats, Small Cats

Objective: Decide which details belong with a main idea.

Materials: Blackline Master 89; pencil

[Answers: Circled: 1, 3, 4, 5, 7, 8]

Distribute Blackline Master 89. Read the directions aloud and discuss them with students. Discuss what makes a detail "belong" with a main idea. Then have students circle the details that belong.

Objective: Add details to an outline.

Materials: Blackline Master 90; pencil

[Answers: Details will vary.]

Distribute copies of Blackline Master 90. Assign pairs of varying levels to work together to complete it. Read the directions aloud, then work with students to think of a detail that might go in the outline, such as *Old building, Grades K-5, Stanley School.* When students have completed their outlines, have them compare details and combine them into a bigger outline on the chalkboard.

Informal Assessment

Have students turn to page 355 in their textbooks. Refer them to Practice A, and have them read item I. in the box. Then have them read item 3. Would this sentence be listed as a detail under the main idea in the box?

Use the following chart to assess and reteach.

Is the student able to: choose the details that belong with a main idea?	Reteach by allowing pre- and early production students to pantomime or draw their responses.
add details to an outline?	Reteach by using the Reteach Activity on TE page 277.

Big Cats, Small Cats

Read the topic and main idea sentence. Should each detail, numbered 1–10, be listed under that main idea? If it should, draw a circle around it.

Topic: Big Cats, Small Cats

I. Lions and tigers are related to the cats we keep as pets.

1. Lions live in groups.

2. Dogs are related to wolves, too.

3. Pet cats need people to help them.

4. Female lions hunt for food.

5. Tigers hunt alone.

6. Cats make my mother sneeze.

7. Lions and pet cats move in similar ways.

8. Tigers have stripes, like lots of house cats.

9. I think lions are the prettiest kind of cats.

10. Most people like either cats better or dogs better.

Name _____ Date _____

School Outline

Make an outline that gives details about your school. Use the form below.

I. My School

A. _____

B. _____

C. _____

D. _____

E. _____

Introduce this lesson before Pupil Edition pages 364–379.

I. PREWRITE
Oral Warm Up

Objectives:
• Explore topic and questions for expository writing.
• Relate information about a topic.

Whole Group Oral Language Activity

Display a picture of a giant panda. Tell students that you know what pandas look like and that they can climb trees. Explain that you would like to know more about pandas. List the following questions on the board: *Where do pandas live? What are their habits? What do they eat?*

Ask students what other questions they might ask about pandas. If possible, allow students to page through books that have pictures of animals. Then ask a volunteer to say which mammal or animal interests him or her, and then have the class brainstorm questions about the subject. For example: Where does it live? Is it a good pet? What does it eat?

Graphic Organizer

Blackline Master 91:
Idea Web

Objectives:
• Use a graphic organizer to prepare an outline.
• Practice writing a topic and questions about a topic.

Materials: Blackline Master 91; pencils

As students suggest questions, help them to create categories: *One student wants to know how fish hear, and another wants to know how fish see. Let's write one question: How do fish use their senses?* Record students' suggestions in a chart.

Introduce the Writing Mode

Explain that expository writing gives information about a subject. Point out that making a list of questions can give a sense of the kinds of information they need to look up in order to write a report.

Scaffolded Writing Instruction

Pre-Production and Early Production

Using Blackline Master 91, have students draw the animals they have chosen for their topics and place them in the top circle. Then have them draw in the circles below three questions they would like to answer about their animals.

Speech Emergence

Have students choose a topic, and draw pictures in the circles. Have them use words and phrases in the spaces below the circles to add to the three questions they have about the topic.

Intermediate and Advanced Fluency

Have students draw pictures and write sentences to name their topics, then write three main questions they have about the topics.

Research and Inquiry: Use an Encyclopedia

Explain that an encyclopedia is a good resource for finding information. Model using the alphabet to choose the correct volume and demonstrate that the subjects in the encyclopedia are arranged alphabetically. Point out the guide words and read the sub-heads for that encyclopedia entry. Then pass the volume of the encyclopedia around the room.

II. DRAFT

Objectives:
- Organize an outline and begin drafting expository writing.
- Add details and questions to an outline.

Focus on Expository Writing

Explain that students can use their charts to make an outline for a report. Point out that every Roman numeral on the outline will be a different paragraph in the finished report. The sentences in each paragraph will answer the questions. Stress that students can use their own knowledge, the information in an encyclopedia, or information in science books to find facts that answer each of their questions.

Scaffolded Writing Instruction

Blackline Master 92: Animal Facts

Ask students to tell what animal they are going to write about, and have the class contribute the information they know about their topics.

Pre-Production & Early Production

Use Blackline Master 92 to help students organize their explanatory work. Have students draw their topic in the square. Then have them add pictures that show any answers they have found for their questions on Blackline Master 91.

Speech Emergence
Blackline Master 93: Animal Report

Using Blackline Master 93, help students create questions in an outline format and give facts about each question in the outline. They will need to use pictures or drawings, and short phrases and words.

Intermediate and Advanced Fluency

Encourage students to add a photo or drawing that shows their topic at the top of the page. Students may begin their expository writing piece. Encourage them to write a sentence that restates each question and then two more sentences to answer it.

III. REVISE

Objectives:
- Revise expository writing.
- Add details and connecting words.

Focus on Elaboration

Write the following sentences on the board and read them aloud with the class: *The bamboo forests are getting smaller. There are very few giant pandas left.*

Tell students that since the pandas have a smaller environment, there are fewer pandas. Stress that this is not your opinion, but a fact. Then add the phrase "Because of this" to the beginning of the second sentence, and explain that the connecting words help clarify the sentences. List the following connecting words: *but, so, at first, later, even though, since, because,* and *also.* Encourage students to use them to connect ideas in their writing.

Scaffolded Instruction for Revising

Pre-Production & Early
Production
Blackline Master 92:
Facts About My Animal

Have students add details to their work by adding to their drawings.
They may also choose one or two words from the list of connecting
words, write them on their drawings, and use arrows to connect them
to the next picture.

Speech Emergence
Blackline Master 93:
Including Facts

Use students' work on Blackline Master 93 to help them add details
with words, phrases, or drawings, and to insert two or three connecting
words between pictures.

Intermediate and Advanced
Fluency

Students may elaborate by adding details to sentences or writing
additional sentences. Ask them to add connecting words that will
relate ideas or sentences. Have students add a concluding sentence,
if they have not already done so.

Technology Link

Have students help each other use an encyclopedia on CD-ROM to
look up information about their subjects.

IV. REVISE • PEER CONFERENCING

Focus on Peer Conferencing

Objectives:
• Participate in peer
conferences.
• Give and receive
suggestions for
improvement.
• Revise expository writing

Pair emerging speakers with pre-production and early production
students. Have them retell what they see and read in their partners'
pictures. Ask questions to help to clarify the information in the pictures.
Pair more fluent speakers to read each others' work. Tell them to follow
the checklist on the board.

Use page 372 as a guide and write a checklist for each language
proficiency level on the chalkboard. Readers can refer to them as they
hold their peer conferences.

V. PROOFREAD

Focus on English Conventions

Objectives:
• Use subject and object
pronouns.
• Practice proofreading
strategies.

Say and write the following sentences, and underline the subject and
object pronouns.

They can hear every sound.

Pandas need help, so people protect them.

Materials: Blackline Master 94;
pencils

[Answers: for Blackline
Master 94: A. 1. she 2. they
3. you 4. it B. 1. her 2. him
3. us 4. them C. 1. I 2. I 3. me
4. I]

Explain that a subject pronoun takes the place of the subject noun of
the sentence. Point to "they" and say that the subject is pandas. Point
to "them" in the second sentence, and explain that this pronoun is an
object pronoun. The plural object pronoun "them" explains "whom or
what" about the verb *protect*.

Have students complete Blackline Master 94 to practice the grammar
skill before proofreading their work.

Explain that proofreading includes checking for spelling mistakes. Begin an "Animal Studies" spelling list on a large piece of paper. On it, write words students have misspelled or want to remember that are related to the animals they have written about.

Point out that a dictionary gives information about how to spell the plural form of a name. For example, the plural of *goose* is *geese*. Explain that an example sentence in a dictionary may also give some information about the subject. For example, an example sentence for geese might say, *The flock of geese landed on the lake.* Model how students could then look up the word *flock* to find that it means "a group of animals." Have a student request the name of an animal, and model how to find it in the dictionary.

VI. PUBLISH

Objective: Present a neat final copy of expository writing and actively view the work of others.

Use page 376 as a guide and write and read aloud a checklist for each language proficiency level. Encourage students to use the checklist as they prepare a final draft.

Extension: Ask volunteers to suggest how to group the reports by subject. Students can then form new groups by subject, and work together to create a table of contents for their part of the book.

Make a Class Book

Have small groups assemble their writing and create a cover and a table of contents. Have more fluent speakers write titles for classmates who need help. Then have groups place their work in a folder to create a class book of "Animal Reports."

VII. LISTENING, SPEAKING, VIEWING, REPRESENTING

Adapt the steps on pages 378–379 to create activities that will bring out the talents of all students. Encourage pre- and early production students to use peer-translators or helpers or to act out their ideas.

Informal Assessment

TPR

When assessing students' learning, you will need to adapt your expectations of what constitutes an appropriate response. For example, you may wish to have students act out or draw a response to a verbal or written prompt rather than having them give a traditional answer.

Have students share their writing, either by reading aloud, or by displaying their drawings and speaking about them. Have non-native speakers first explain their drawings in their own languages, and then in English.

Name_____ Date_____

Idea Web

Think about the animal you will report on. Draw the animal. Then draw or write three questions you have about the animal.

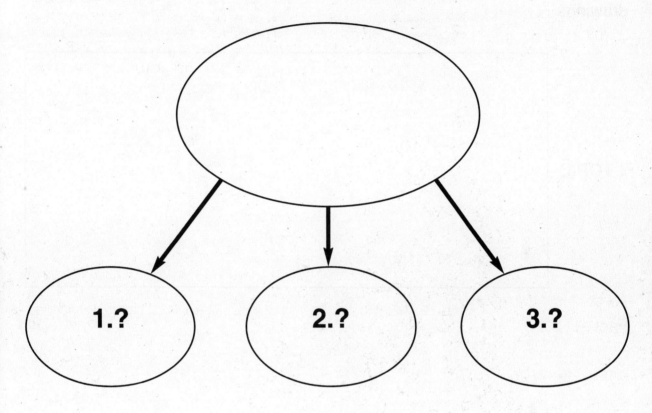

1.? _____

2.? _____

3.? _____

Name_____ Date_____

Animal Facts

Draw the animal you want for the topic of your report. Draw pictures to show three facts about the animal. Remember to use details in your drawings.

TOPIC

Fact 1:

_____

Fact 2:

_____

Fact 3:

Name_____ Date_____

Animal Report

Draw or write the topic of your report. Write the three questions you will answer. Give two facts that answer each question. Then add words, phrases, and sentences. Remember to include details in your pictures.

TOPIC

Question 1:

Fact:

Fact:

Question 2:

Fact:

Fact:

Question 3:

Fact:

Fact:

Subject and Object Pronouns

A. Draw a line under the subject pronoun in each sentence.

1. She went to the bird house to see the parrots.

2. They were very noisy.

3. You should come with us next time.

4. It is a great trip.

B. Write the object pronoun to complete the sentence correctly.

1. Zack spilled his juice all over (she, her) _____.

2. I thought Claire would be mad at (he, him) _____.

3. Mr. Lee bought some popcorn for (we, us) _____.

4. The birds thought the popcorn was for (them, they) _____.

C. Write the subject pronoun *I* or the object pronoun *me* to complete the sentence.

1. _____ went to the zoo yesterday. (I, me)

2. My brother and _____ like animals. (I, me)

3. I feel sad when animals look at _____. (I, me)

4. _____ wish they didn't have to be in cages. (I, me)

ADJECTIVES THAT TELL *WHAT KIND*

I. DEVELOP ORAL LANGUAGE
Oral Focus on Grammar Skill

Objective: Orally describe pictures and identify nouns and adjectives that tell *what kind.*

Whole Group Oral Language Activity

Show students photographs or pictures of several objects, such as an elephant, a boat, a house, a plate of food. Ask: *What word can describe the (elephant)?* (huge) Write *huge elephant* on the chalkboard.

Remind students that an adjective is a word that describes a noun. Point to the words you wrote on the chalkboard. Ask a volunteer to say which word is the adjective, and then the noun. Because the position of adjectives in other languages is often different from English conventions, be sure to point out that an adjective usually comes before a noun. Then invite students to take turns round-robin style describing the elephant with one or more adjectives *(big, gray, rough, heavy, scary, funny, smart).* Repeat with the other pictures.

Scaffolded Verbal Prompting

Use the following verbal prompts to help students better understand adjectives that tell what kind.

Nonverbal Prompt for Active Participation

Pre-Production: *Point to the picture of the elephant. Show how big the elephant is.*

One- or Two-Word Response Prompt

Early Production: *Say an adjective you see on the chalkboard. Now tell me what noun it describes.*

Prompt for Short Answers to Higher-Level Thinking Skills

Speech Emergence: *What does an adjective do for a noun? Name a noun and its adjective. Now give me a different adjective to describe the same noun.*

Prompt for Detailed Answers to Higher-Level Thinking Skills

Intermediate and Advanced Fluency: *Explain in a sentence what kind of adjective this is:* huge. *Now name a noun it can describe. Tell me a sentence using that adjective and noun.*

II. DEVELOP GRAMMAR SKILLS IN CONTEXT
Visual/Physical Focus on Grammar Skill

Objective: Develop and demonstrate understanding of adjectives that tell *what kind.*

Blackline Master 95

[**Possible answers:** beautiful [rose], fast [train], long [snake], round [ball], soft [pillow], empty [basket]]

TPR

Whole Group Activity

Show a large picture of an object, such as a *lighthouse.* Write a few adjectives on the chalkboard, such as *tall, important, old, exciting, funny.* Include a couple of adjectives that do not describe the lighthouse. Draw a line. Ask a student to choose a word that describes the lighthouse and write it on the line. Draw another line and ask another student to write another word to describe the lighthouse. Repeat. Then ask the class to vote on the adjective they like best. Say: *If you like (tall) jump up. If you like (old), scratch your head. And so on.*

Distribute Blackline Master 95 to students. Have them complete the page independently by cutting out the adjectives and placing them next to the pictures. Then take a class poll to see how many students chose the same adjectives.

Small Group Activity

Have groups look at Blackline Master 95 together. Ask them to vote on which adjective to choose for each picture, then complete the page. Groups can compare and give reasons for their answers.

Partner Activity

Extension: Have students make another list of adjectives and choose new descriptions for the pictures on Blackline Master 95.

Partners make their adjective choices independently and then compare answers. Then have partners take turns drawing other pictures that the adjectives on Blackline Master 95 might describe and choosing adjectives for the new pictures.

Technology Link

Extension: Have students use the format on Blackline Master 95 to list a few adjectives that tell what kind and draw several pictures that might go with the adjectives. Then give the page to other students, who choose pictures to match the adjectives.

Guide students to a web site that has some text. Pair students and ask them to read a section of text and write all the adjectives that tell what kind. Then students can enter the adjectives into a class database of adjectives that tell what kind.

III. PRACTICE GRAMMAR SKILLS
Written Focus on Grammar Skill

Use the following Blackline Masters to reinforce unit grammar skills.

Introduce Blackline Master 96: School Picnic Fun

Objective: Identify and write adjectives and the nouns they describe.

Materials: Blackline Master 96; pen or pencil; crayons or colored pencils

[Answers: adjectives: great, delicious, interesting, sunny, wonderful; nouns: picnic, food, games, sky, day]

Form student pairs. Distribute Blackline Master 96. Read aloud and discuss the directions with students. Ask: *How do you know which words are adjectives?* (They describe or tell *what kind* about the noun.) Have students read the paragraph aloud with you. Then tell partners to complete the exercise. Invite students to explain and display their drawings.

Informal Assessment

Have students look at the picture on page 398. Ask: What adjectives can you think of that tell *what kind?* Have students make a list of the adjectives and nouns they think of.

Introduce Blackline Master 97: *What Kind* of Travels?

Objective: Place adjectives in a word web and write a story with the adjectives and nouns.

Materials: Blackline Master 97; pen or pencil

[Possible answers: places: exciting, hot; food: tasty, strange; people: friendly; clothing: colorful, strange]

Make a word web on the chalkboard with *country* in the center circle. Say: *Help me think of a few adjectives that tell what kind of country.* Write the adjectives in the word web (far, interesting, big). Then invite students to each write a sentence using an adjective and *country,* for example, *China is a big country.* Then give each student a copy of Blackline Master 97. Read the directions with students. Ask them to work with a partner to complete the word web and write a story about Marco Polo's travels.

Informal Assessment

Read some sentences aloud from More Practice on page 399. Ask students to name the adjectives and the nouns they describe.

Use the following chart to assess and reteach.

Are students able to:	
orally identify adjectives that tell what kind?	Reteach by working with students orally on Reteach BLM 75 on TE page 399.
pair adjectives with the nouns they describe?	Reteach using the Language Support Activity on TE page 398.
write sentences with adjectives that tell what kind?	Reteach using the Reteach Activity on TE page 399.

Describe That Picture!

Read the adjectives and look at the pictures. Choose one adjective to tell *what kind* for each picture. Cut out the adjective and paste or glue it next to the picture.

soft	empty	round	fast
beautiful	hot	long	tall

Name_____ Date_____

School Picnic Fun

Read the paragraph. Write the adjectives and nouns in the chart below.
Draw a picture in the box of one scene from the paragraph.

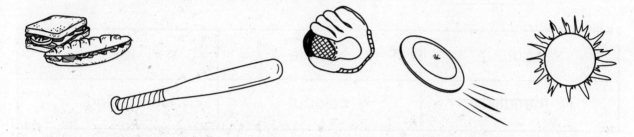

We had a great picnic yesterday. Everyone brought delicious food.
We played interesting games under a sunny sky. What a wonderful day!

Adjectives that Tell What Kind	Nouns They Describe

What Kind of Travels?

Read the list of adjectives and the word web. Write the adjectives in the word web.

hot	strange	tasty
friendly	colorful	exciting

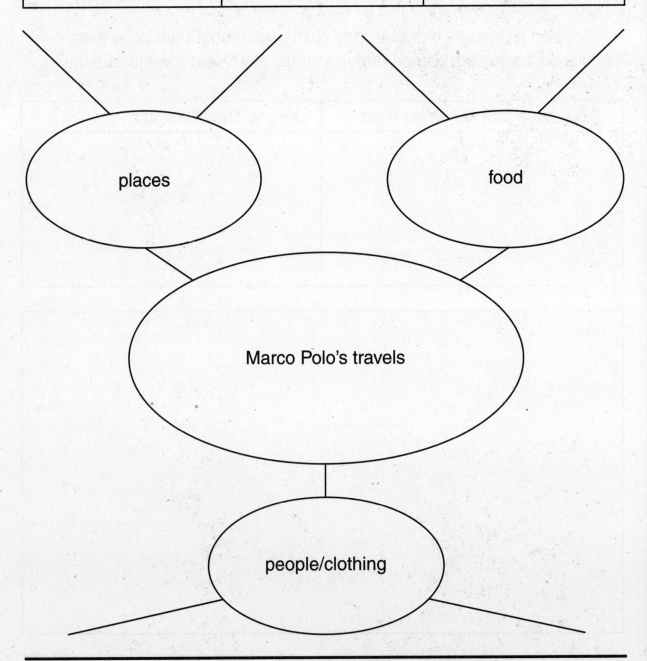

ADJECTIVES THAT TELL *HOW MANY*

I. DEVELOP ORAL LANGUAGE
Oral Focus on Grammar Skill

Objective: Classify and identify examples of adjectives that tell how many about the verb.

Whole Group Oral Language Activity

Refer students to the picture of the parrots on page 400. Write *how many?* on the chalkboard. Ask: *How many parrots are in the picture?* Count the parrots aloud with students. Write *seven parrots* on the chalkboard and have students say the phrase with you. Then tell students that *seven* is an adjective that tells how many parrots. Point out that adjectives that tell how many always come before the noun.

Then write *few, many*, and *several* on the chalkboard. Say: *There are several parrots in the picture.* Then tell students to cover four of the parrots with their hands. Ask: *How many parrots do you see?* Prompt them to answer both *three* and a *few*. Have partners place their books next to each other with both pictures of the parrots in a line. Ask: *How many parrots do you see?* Prompt students to answer both *14* and *many*. Repeat the exercise, with students answering in complete sentences.

Scaffolded Verbal Prompting

Use the following verbal prompts to help students better understand adjectives that tell how many.

Nonverbal Prompt for Active Participation

Pre-Production: *Look at the parrots. Hold up your fingers to tell how many there are. Cover four parrots with your hand. How many are there now?*

One- or Two-Word Response Prompt

Early Production: *Tell me how many parrots are in the picture. Cover three parrots with your hand. How many are there now? Repeat the correct sentence:* I have parrots two. I have two parrots.

Prompt for Short Answers to Higher-Level Thinking Skills

Speech Emergence: *Count the parrots and tell me in a sentence how many there are. Choose one of these words and tell me in a sentence how many there are—*few, several, many. *Does the adjective come before or after the noun?*

Prompt for Detailed Answers to Higher-Level Thinking Skills

Intermediate and Advanced Fluency: *Say a sentence that tells about how many parrots there are, and a sentence that tells exactly how many parrots there are. Where do adjectives that tell how many belong? Where does the noun belong?*

II. DEVELOP GRAMMAR SKILLS IN CONTEXT
Visual/Physical Focus on Grammar Skill

Objective: Develop and demonstrate understanding of adjectives that tell how many.

Blackline Master 98

[Answers: several turtles (6); a few turtles (3); one turtle (1); many turtles (9)]

TPR

Extension: Have students write sentences using their *few, several,* and *many* phrases.

Extension: Have students classify the items in different categories, such as *things for dogs, food, pet homes.* Then ask students to write sentences that tell how many of each category.

Whole Group Activity

Write *a few stars* on the chalkboard. Explain that *a few* usually means three or four. Invite a volunteer to draw three or four stars next to the words. Then write *several stars.* Explain that *several* usually means five to seven. Ask a volunteer to draw several stars next to the words. Finally, write *many* stars and tell students that *many* usually refers to more than seven. Have a volunteer draw many stars on the chalkboard.

Make a chart on the chalkboard like this one:

a few	three or four
several	five to seven
many	eight or more

Draw the appropriate number of stars in each row of the left column to illustrate the adjectives.

Give a copy of Blackline Master 98 to each student. Read the directions together and have students complete the page.

Small Group Activity

Have each group of three students make a set of three cards with drawings: three, six, and ten of whatever animal they want. Then call out *a few, several,* and *many* in random order and have students with the corresponding cards stand and hold them up. Then have students regroup in three groups for *few, several,* and *many.* Have groups write phrases that describe all their cards, such as *three monkeys, three flamingos,* and so on. Students can read their lists of phrases aloud to the class.

Partner Activity

Give partners a list of several items—each printed on a separate card —that they might find in a pet store, for example, *fish tank, bird cage, dog collar, leash, bag of cat litter.* Then give them the same number of cards that say *few, several, many, two, four, seven,* and so on. Have partners take turns drawing one card of each kind, adjective and noun. Students put the two cards together in a phrase, write the phrase, and draw the number of the item indicated.

Technology Link

Have students log on to **www.mhschool.com/language-arts** and go to a page or link that has some text. Students skim the text for adjectives that tell how many and take turns reading the sentences that contain them aloud to each other.

III. PRACTICE GRAMMAR SKILLS
Written Focus on Grammar Skill

Use the following Blackline Masters to reinforce unit grammar skills.

Introduce Blackline Master 99: What's in the Pet Shop?

Objective: Match adjectives with nouns and write the phrases in sentences.

Materials: Blackline Master 99; pen or pencil

[Answers: a few dog dishes; many leashes; several aquariums; two bags of litter; nine cans of cat food, one dog sweater; 1) many leashes; 2) nine cans of cat food; 3) a few dog dishes; 4) one dog sweater; 5) several aquariums; 6) two bags of litter]

Put countable items on a desk or table, such as three books, nine pencils, one stapler. Ask students to count the items with you as you write the number and name of the item on the chalkboard. Then write sentences with blanks for the adjectives and nouns: We have _____ to write with. Ask volunteers to fill in the blanks. Then distribute Blackline Master 99. Read aloud and discuss the directions with students. Have partners complete the page. Then ask students to read the sentences aloud.

Informal Assessment

Read some sentences aloud from Guided Practice on page 400. Ask students to repeat the adjective that tells how many and name the noun that it describes. Then tell students to write the phrases.

Introduce Blackline Master 100: Aquarium Project

Objective: Match adjectives and nouns in the correct order and complete sentences with them.

Materials: Blackline Master 100; pen or pencil

[Answers: 1. a few bags; 2. five strands; 3. one diver; 4. several rocks; 5. two logs; 6. many guppies]

Display a picture or poster that contains countable items. On the chalkboard, write a few separate adjectives and nouns that tell about things in the picture. Ask volunteers to match adjectives with nouns and write the phrases on the chalkboard. Read them aloud in sentences that tell about the picture. Then pass out copies of Blackline Master 100. After students have read the directions, have partners complete the exercise. Allow pairs to compare their answers with other pairs and discuss any differences.

Informal Assessment

Take a few sentences from More Practice on page 401 and write them in scrambled word order on the chalkboard. Have students arrange the words correctly and identify adjectives and nouns.

Use the following chart to assess and reteach.

Are students able to:	
orally identify adjectives that tell how many and the nouns they describe?	Reteach using the Language Support Activity on TE page 400.
put adjectives and nouns in the correct order?	Reteach by working with students orally on Reteach BLM 76 on TE page 401.
use *a few, several,* and *many* correctly?	Reteach using the Reteach Activity on TE page 401.

How Many Turtles?

Look at the pictures and read the words in the boxes. Cut out the pictures and glue or paste them in the correct box.

Several turtles	A few turtles
One turtle	Many turtles

Name_____ Date_____

What's in the Pet Shop?

Look at the pictures and choose the adjective that goes with each one. Write the adjective under the picture. Then write the phrases in the sentences below.

many	several	A few
two	one	nine

_____ dog dishes	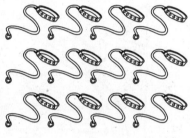 _____ leashes	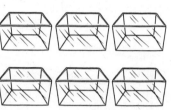 _____ aquariums
 _____ bags of litter	 _____ cans of cat food	 _____ dog sweater

1. There are _____ to take dogs on walks.

2. I see _____ for hungry cats.

3. There are _____ for hungry dogs.

4. The pet shop has only _____ left.

5. It has _____ for fish.

6. People can buy _____ for their cat boxes.

Name_____ Date_____

Aquarium Project

Read the sentences about the things in the picture. Choose an adjective and a noun from the list and write them in the blanks.

guppies	a few	one	logs	two	bags
rocks	several	strands	diver	many	five

Alexis and Adam set up their new aquarium.

1. Adam spread _____ _____ of gravel in the bottom.

2. Alexis put _____ _____ of seaweed in the corner.

3. They both chose _____ _____ to sit on the bottom.

4. Alexis found _____ _____ to place in the tank.

5. Adam wanted _____ _____ for the fish to hide in.

6. They both chose _____ _____ to swim in the aquarium.

ADJECTIVES THAT COMPARE

I. DEVELOP ORAL LANGUAGE
Oral Focus on Grammar Skill

Objective: Classify adjectives that compare by ending.

TPR

Whole Group Oral Language Activity

Make a set of cards, a different one for each student, with a variety of adjectives that compare, such as *wider, tallest, heavier, bigger, bluest, oldest.* Write these headings on the chalkboard: *-er, -est, -ier, -iest.* Then say and write a sentence with each adjective, such as *The Mississippi River is wider than the Salmon River.* Ask: *Who has the card with the adjective that compares in that sentence? Jump up and say "Bingo!"* Tell the student to bring his or her card to the chalkboard, set it on the tray under the correct heading, and say the word aloud. Have the class repeat and spell the word aloud. Continue with the other words.

Scaffolded Verbal Prompting

Use the following verbal prompts to help students better understand adjectives that compare.

Nonverbal Prompt for Active Participation

Pre-Production: (Ask two students of different heights to stand up.) *Point to the taller one. Point to the shorter one.* [Ask another student to stand next to the other two.) *Tap the shoulder of the tallest one. Shake hands with the shortest one.*

One- or Two-Word Response Prompt

Early Production: *Tell me the adjective that compares in this sentence:* Maria is taller than Joe. *Name the two people that it compares.*

Prompt for Short Answers to Higher-Level Thinking Skills

Speech Emergence: *Read me a sentence from the chalkboard that has an adjective that ends in -est. In -er. What are the two adjectives that compare for* (wide)?

Prompt for Detailed Answers to Higher-Level Thinking Skills

Intermediate and Advanced Fluency: *Tell me the rule for changing the spelling of the two adjectives that compare for* (big). *How do you decide whether to add* -er *or* -est *to an adjective to compare nouns?*

II. DEVELOP GRAMMAR SKILLS IN CONTEXT
Visual/Physical Focus on Grammar Skill

Objective: Develop and demonstrate understanding of adjectives that compare.

Blackline Master 101

TPR

Whole Group Activity

Ask students to color or draw a decorative border around each card on Blackline Master 101. Have them cut the cards apart. Divide the class into two teams. Write several sentences on the board in this format: *She is the _____ runner in the race. (fast)* Include examples of all the possible endings for adjectives that compare. Call on the first student in team 1 to hold up the card with the correct ending. If he or she does so, that student says and writes the adjective in the blank. The same team gets another turn until a student gives an incorrect answer, then the other team takes a turn. Continue until all students have had a turn.

Small Group Activity

Give each group a list of nouns and adjectives from the exercises on pages 404–407. Have students turn their ending cards over and take turns drawing one. Students must then choose a noun and appropriate adjective from the list and change the adjective to that comparative ending.

Extension: Have students write a sentence using each noun and comparative adjective they choose.

Partner Activity

Partners can use the same list of nouns and adjectives from the textbook exercises. One partner chooses a noun and adjective and hands the other student any ending card. That student either changes the adjective to the ending indicated or says that it's incorrect. If it's incorrect, the second student chooses another card until he or she finds one with an ending that is correct with the adjective. Partners change roles.

Extension: Challenge partners to make a chart of all the adjective and noun phrases in the five ending categories.

Technology Link

Using the table function in a word processor, have students make a chart, with space to add more words, of all the adjective and noun phrases in the five ending categories. Encourage them to add to the chart as they read and encounter more adjectives that compare.

III. PRACTICE GRAMMAR SKILLS
Written Focus on Grammar Skill

Use the following Blackline Masters to reinforce unit grammar skills.

Introduce Blackline Master 102: Comparisons and Rules

Review the comparative forms with students and the rules for spelling changes on pages 404 and 406. Distribute Blackline Master 102. Read aloud and discuss the directions with students. Work through the first item together with students. They can copy the rules from their textbooks. Then ask them to make up oral sentences for each form with the nouns in the picture (man).

Objective: Write comparative forms and provide rules for spelling changes.

Materials: Blackline Master 102; pen or pencil

[**Answers:** stronger, strongest; rules: Add *–er* to an adjective to compare two nouns. Add *–est* to compare more than two nouns. thinner, thinnest; rule: For adjectives that have a single vowel sound before a final consonant, double the final consonant and add *–er* or *–est*.
busier, busiest; rule: When the adjective ends in a consonant sound and *y,* change the *y* to *i* and add *–er* or *–est.*
cuter, cutest; rule: When the adjective ends in *e,* drop the *e* and add *–er* or *–est.*]

Informal Assessment

Turn to page 405 and read a sentence aloud. On the chalkboard, write the adjective in parentheses. Then reread the sentence with either the comparative or the superlative form of the adjective. Call on students to write that comparative form on paper, then check answers.

Introduce Blackline Master 103: Adjective Puzzles

Give students several adjectives that compare in two pieces, with the beginnings and endings on separate slips of paper. Ask students to pair the slips that go together and read the words aloud. Then give students a copy of Blackline Master 103. Read the directions. Have students complete the exercise independently and then share their sentences.

Informal Assessment

Objective: Join comparative endings to adjectives and write sentences using them.

Materials: Blackline Master 103; pen or pencil

[**Answers:** quieter, quietest; lazier, laziest; bluer, bluest; fatter, fattest]

Write some adjectives from More Practice on page 407 in this form: *funny → funny + i + er = funnier,* but leave some blanks in the "equation." Have students fill in the blanks.

Use the following chart to assess and reteach.

Are students able to:	
say the comparative forms of adjectives?	Reteach using the Language Support Activity on TE page 404.
change the spelling of adjectives to comparative forms?	Reteach using the Reteach Activity on TE page 407.
write phrases with adjectives that compare and nouns?	Reteach using the Reteach Activity on TE page 405.

Grade 3

Unit 6 • GRAMMAR/Adjectives That Compare **215**

-er

-est

-ier/-iest

Drop the *e* and add *-er* or *-est*.

Double the final consonant and add *-er* or *-est*.

Comparisons and Rules

Look at each row of pictures. On the lines, write the adjectives that compare. Then write the rule.

strong _____ _____

Rule:

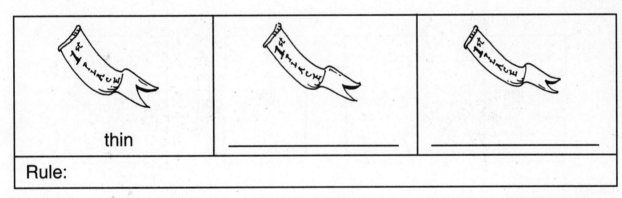

thin _____ _____

Rule:

busy _____ _____

Rule:

cute _____ _____

Rule:

Adjective Puzzles

Cut out the puzzle pieces. Put the pieces together in the correct order in each box. On the line, write a sentence using one of the adjectives and the noun in parentheses.

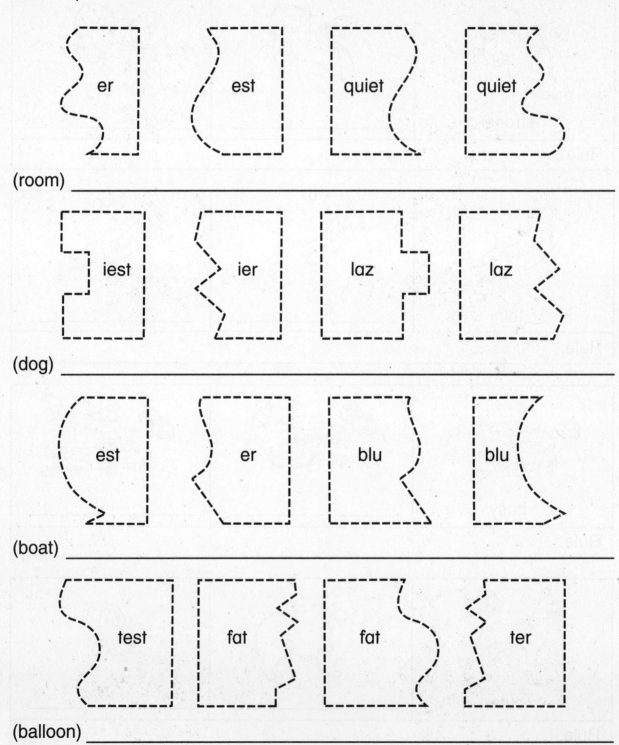

(room) _____

(dog) _____

(boat) _____

(balloon) _____

ADVERBS THAT TELL
HOW, WHEN, WHERE

I. DEVELOP ORAL LANGUAGE
Oral Focus on Grammar Skill

Objective: Classify adverbs as telling how, when, or where about the verb.

Whole Group Oral Language Activity

Divide the class into three sections. Give each section a word to say: *how, when, where.* Write some adverb/verb phrases on the chalkboard, such as *search everywhere, always eats, walk briskly.* Read one phrase, point to the verb, and have students identify it aloud as a verb with you. *(Search is a verb.)* Do the same for the adverb. Then ask: *Does the adverb tell how, when, or where about the verb?* Prompt the appropriate section to call out their word in unison.

Explain that adverbs can come before or after a verb in a sentence. Write the following sentence on the chalkboard: *Mom made sandwiches for lunch yesterday.* Have students say it with you. Then prompt students to answer in complete sentences as you ask: *What is the verb? (made) What is the adverb? (yesterday)* Explain that this adverb comes after the verb. Ask: *What does this adverb tell about the verb? (when)* Repeat with other sentences that show adverbs that tell how, when, and where both before and after the verb. Point out that adverbs that tell *how* often end in *ly (quickly).*

Scaffolded Verbal Prompting

TPR

Use the following verbal prompts to help students better understand adverbs that tell how, when, where.

Nonverbal Prompt for Active Participation

Pre-Production: *Show me how to walk slowly. Listen as I say a sentence about what you are doing: You walk slowly. Raise your hand when you hear the word that tells how you walk.*

One- or Two-Word Response Prompt

Early Production: *Tell me the verb in this sentence. Now tell me the adverb. Does the adverb come before or after the verb? Say an adverb and verb phrase in which the adverb tells (how).*

Prompt for Short Answers to Higher-Level Thinking Skills

Speech Emergence: *What does an adverb do? Name an adverb you see on the chalkboard that tells (when). What verb does it tell more about?*

Prompt for Detailed Answers to Higher-Level Thinking Skills

Intermediate and Advanced Fluency: *What is an adverb? How do you know which adverbs tell how? Name the adverb and verb in this sentence. State in a sentence whether the adverb tells how, when, or where.*

II. DEVELOP GRAMMAR SKILLS IN CONTEXT
Visual/Physical Focus on Grammar Skill

Objective: Develop and demonstrate understanding of adverbs that tell how, when, or where.

Blackline Master 104

TPR

Whole Group Activity

Give each student a copy of Blackline Master 104 and have them color or decorate the cards and cut them out.

Write a few simple sentences with adverbs that tell how, when, and where. Cut the words apart, one to a card. Mix up the cards for one sentence and place them on the chalk tray. Ask students to help you unscramble the sentence and place the cards in the correct order. Then ask: *What is the verb? What is the adverb?* Have volunteers come up and hold up first the verb card then the adverb card. Then ask: *What does the adverb tell about the verb?* Allow a volunteer to bring up the appropriate card from Blackline Master 104 and hold it next to the adverb card. Repeat with other sentences.

Small Group Activity

Give students several cards with adverbs written on them. Have the group brainstorm a verb to go with each adverb. Then have students use their cards from Blackline Master 104 as list headings and place the adverb/verb cards in piles under the appropriate headings.

TPR

Extension: Have students act out for another group as many adverb/verb phrases as possible. Groups can guess each other's pantomimes and check them against their adverb/verb cards.

Extension: Partners can collaborate on writing a paragraph or longer story using as many of their adverb/phrases as they can.

Partner Activity

Have each partner brainstorm a few adverbs for each category (how, when, where). Then tell partners to exchange lists and supply a verb to go with each adverb. Then have them read the verb/adverb phrases aloud to each other.

Technology Link

Have students create an "adverb web page" in which they give rules, examples, and exercises for adverbs that tell how, when, and where. Encourage them to use catchy phrases, charts, and any graphics your computer software may be capable of.

III. PRACTICE GRAMMAR SKILLS
Written Focus on Grammar Skill

Use the following Blackline Masters to reinforce unit grammar skills.

Introduce Blackline Master 105: Sort the Adverbs

Objective: Classify adverbs as how, when, or where.

Materials: Blackline Master 105; scissors, glue or paste

[Answers: how: easily, wildly, loudly; when: first, next, today; where: there, nearby, ahead]

For review, call out a few adverbs from the lesson and have students respond with *how, when,* or *where.* Then give each student a copy of Blackline Master 105. Read the directions together. Have students complete the activity alone and exchange it with a partner to correct. Ask: *What do you notice about all the adverbs that tell how?* (They end in -ly.)

Informal Assessment

Have students suggest another adverb for each one in More Practice on page 413.

Introduce Blackline Master 106: Sentences with Adverbs

Objective: Use adverbs in original sentences using pictures as prompts.

Materials: Blackline Master 106; pen or pencil

[Answers: sentences should include in this order: early, slowly, everywhere, suddenly, fast, downstairs]

Distribute Blackline Master 106. Read aloud and discuss the directions with students. Tell students to use the pictures for clues as they write their sentences. Have students complete the exercise in pairs, then read their sentences to another pair of students. For more work, have students categorize the adverbs as telling how, when, or where.

Informal Assessment

Give students a list of paired adverbs and verbs from sentences in More Practice on page 415 and 417. Ask them to choose one way to show they understand what the adverb does: 1) pantomime the action, 2) draw a picture of the action, 3) say what the action is and whether the adverb tells how, when, or where.

Use the following chart to assess and reteach.

Are students able to: identify adverbs?	Reteach using the Language Support Activity on TE pages 412, 414, and 416.
put adverbs and verbs together appropriately?	Reteach using the Extend Activity on TE page 413.
classify adverbs as telling how, when or where?	Reteach using the Reteach Activity on TE pages 413, 415, and 417.

how

when

where

Name_____ Date_____

Sort the Adverbs

Read the adverb inside each ⬭ . Cut them out and glue or paste them in the correct nest.

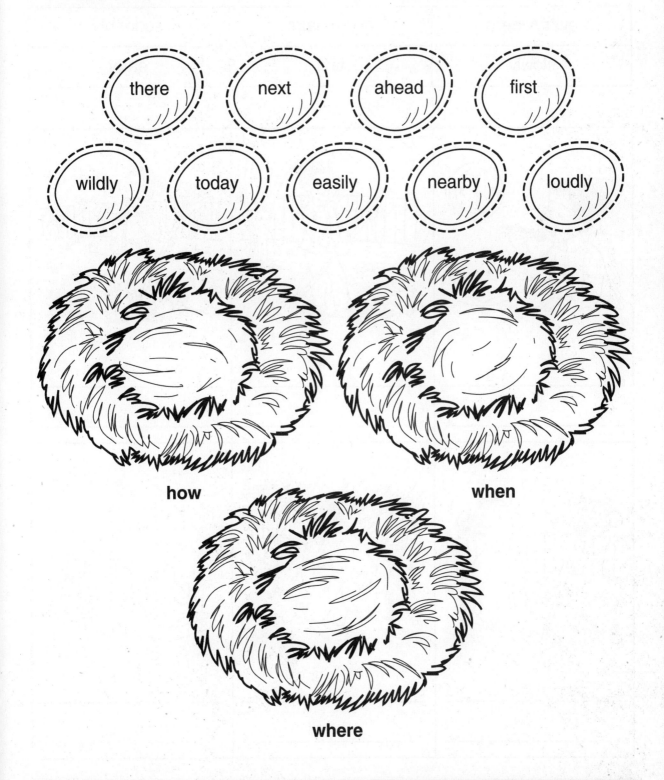

there   next   ahead   first

wildly   today   easily   nearby   loudly

how   when

where

Sentences with Adverbs

Read the list of adverbs and look at the pictures. Write a sentence about each picture. Use an adverb from the list.

everywhere	downstairs	suddenly
slowly	fast	early

SYNONYMS AND ANTONYMS

Introduce this lesson before Pupil Edition pages 434–435.

I. DEVELOP ORAL LANGUAGE
Oral Focus on Vocabulary Skill

Objective: Identify, generate, and use synonyms and antonyms.

Whole Group Oral Language Activity

Show a picture of a street or point to a street outside the classroom. Say: *This is a street. What are some other names we call streets? (roads, highways, lanes, avenues, boulevards, etc.) All of these other words are synonyms for* street. Discuss what red and green traffic lights tell drivers to do. Explain that *stop* and *go* are antonyms, they mean opposite things. Discuss other opposites.

Scaffolded Verbal Prompting

Use the following verbal prompts to help students better understand synonyms and antonyms.

Nonverbal Prompt for Active Participation

Pre-Production: Say: *Act out these two synonyms. First act sick. Now act ill. Let's act out these antonyms. First stand up. Now sit down.*

T-PR
One- or Two-Word Response Prompt

Early Production: *Which is a synonym for loud: quiet or noisy? (noisy) Name an antonym for difficult. (easy)*

Prompt for Short Answers to Higher-Level Thinking Skills

Speech Emergence: *Are* warm *and* cool *synonyms or antonyms? Tell how you know. (antonyms because they mean the opposite)*

Prompt for Detailed Answers to Higher-Level Thinking Skills

Intermediate and Advanced Fluency: *Name a synonym and an antonym for* little. *Tell how you know which is which.*

II. DEVELOP VOCABULARY SKILLS IN CONTEXT
Visual/Physical Focus on Vocabulary Skill

Objective: Identify and generate synonyms and antonyms.

Small Group Activity

Give each group index cards to make up game cards about synonyms and antonyms. Each card should ask a question. For example: *What are two synonyms for pretty?* or *What word is an antonym for dirty?* Below each question, the student should write possible answers. Have groups challenge each other in a synonym/antonym bee.

Technology Link

Show students how to use an electronic Thesaurus on CD-ROM or on the Internet to find synonyms or antonyms.

Partner Activity

Have partners make finger puppets or paper bag puppets. Tell partners to put on a puppet show about a trip to a special place. Their puppet's dialogue should contain at least three synonym pairs and three antonym pairs. Have students write on a sheet of paper the pairs that they use. As the partners put on their play, have audience members listen for the synonyms and antonyms and name the pairs they heard.

III. PRACTICE VOCABULARY SKILLS
Written Focus on Vocabulary Skill

Objective: Identify words as synonyms or antonyms.

Materials: Blackline Master 107; pencils

[**Answers:** 1: S; 2: A; 3: A; 4: S; 5: S; 6: A]

Introduce Blackline Master 107: Find Synonyms and Antonyms

Distribute Blackline Master 107. Review the meaning of the terms *synonym* and *antonym* and have students discuss examples, such as *big/large* and *off/on.* Read the directions with students and then complete the first example with them. Direct students' attention to the trees in the first picture. Ask a volunteer to read the two words next to the picture. Discuss with students whether the words mean about the same thing or if they mean opposite things. Remind students to write *S* for synonym and *A* for antonym. Have students write their answers on the line. Check student's work. Then have students complete the rest of the exercises.

Objective: Identify synonyms and antonyms.

Materials: Blackline Master 108; pencils

[**Answers:** 1: wishes, needs; 2: good, lovely; 3: runs, races; 4: short, little]

Introduce Blackline Master 108: Synonym and Antonym Choices

Distribute Blackline Master 108. Read the directions and then complete the first example with them. Read the sentences to exercise 1 to students. Ask students what they need to find. Tell students to circle the two words that mean about the same as *wants.* Check students' work. Then have students complete the rest of the exercises. Remind students that for exercises 3 and 4 they need to find antonyms.

Informal Assessment

Have students turn to page 435 in the textbook. Refer them to exercise one in Practice A. Ask, *How do you know that* smart *and* clever *mean about the same thing? (They both mean that you know things.)* Next, read aloud exercise 6 in Practice B. Ask, *How can you show that* short *and* long *are antonyms? (Possible answer: you can use your hands.)*

Use the following chart to assess and reteach.

Are students able to:	
use synonyms and antonyms to describe objects?	Reteach by using the Language Support Activity on TE page 434.
generate a synonym or antonym for a given word?	Reteach by using the Reteach Activity on TE page 435.

Find Synonyms and Antonyms

Look at each picture. Read the two words. Write **S** if the words are synonyms. Write **A** if the two words are antonyms.

1.   high   tall

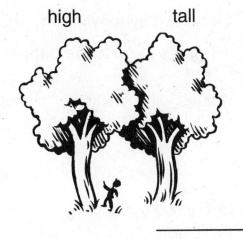

_____

2.   young   old

_____

3.   smooth   bumpy

_____

4.   wagon   cart

_____

5.   sack   bag

_____

6.   wet   dry

_____

Synonym and Antonym Choices

Look at each picture. Read each sentence. Circle the words that are synonyms or antonyms for each underlined word.

1.

Circle two synonyms.

Jill <u>wants</u> to go to the park.

wishes   walks   hopes

2.

Circle two synonyms.

It is a <u>nice</u> day.

bad   good   lovely

3.

Circle two antonyms.

Jill <u>walks</u> to the swings.

runs   races   falls

4.

Circle two antonyms.

Jill swings for a <u>long</u> time.

short   good   little

BEGINNING, MIDDLE, END

Introduce this lesson before Pupil Edition pages 436–437.

I. DEVELOP ORAL LANGUAGE
Oral Focus on Composition Skill

Objective: Orally tell a story with a beginning, middle, and end.

Whole Group Oral Language Activity

Have children look at the photograph of the boy in cowboy clothes on page 437. Ask them to think of a story they might make up about him. How would they begin their story? What would they tell in the middle? How would they end the story? Have students act out the story to show what happens.

Scaffolded Verbal Prompting

Use the following verbal prompts to help students understand beginning, middle, and end.

Nonverbal Prompt for Active Participation

Pre-Production: *Show me something the boy in the cowboy suit might do at the beginning of a story.*

One- or Two-Word Response Prompt

Early Production: *Tell me one thing in the picture that would give you an idea for a sentence in the story.*

Prompt for Short Answers to Higher-Level Thinking Skills

Speech Emergence: *Make up a beginning sentence for a story about the boy in the picture.*

Prompt for Detailed Answers to Higher-Level Thinking Skills

Intermediate and Advanced Fluency: *Look at the picture. In a sentence, tell me something that might happen in the middle of the story about the boy. What might he do?*

II. DEVELOP COMPOSITION SKILLS IN CONTEXT
Visual/Physical Focus on Composition Skill

Extension: Have students make a cartoon strip version of the story about the boy in the picture.

Objective: Complete a story by thinking of a middle and an end.

TPR

Small Group Activity

Give each group an index card with a story starter on it. Example: *On Tuesday, I rode a horse for the first time.* Have students work together to come up with the rest of the story. Remind them that they have the beginning, so they need to think of a middle and an end.

Technology Link

Have students type their stories into a word processing program. Remind them that they can re-order their sentences to make a better story by using the cut and paste feature.

Extension: Have students find a book or story they like. Ask them to read the first sentence aloud and explain why they think it makes a good beginning.

Partner Activity

Have each partner write three sentences that could come in the middle of a story about a day at a school event, then exchange papers. Challenge the partner to write a beginning and an end.

III. PRACTICE COMPOSITION SKILLS
Written Focus on Composition Skill

Objective:
• Identify sentences that come at the beginning or end of a story.

Materials: Blackline Master 109; pencil

[**Answers:** Beginning box: 1, 4, 5, 7, 8, 10]

Objective:
• Write beginning and end sentences for a story.

Materials: Blackline Master 110; pencil

[**Answers:** Sentences will vary.]

Introduce Blackline Master 109: Beginning or End?

Distribute Blackline Master 109. Discuss what kinds of information you usually find at the beginning of a story and what kinds you find at the end. *How do the sentences differ?* Read the directions aloud with students. Make sure they understand that they are to place the number of the sentence in the corresponding box.

Introduce Blackline Master 110: Finish the Story

Distribute Blackline Master 110. Have students work in pairs of varying levels to do this exercise. Review what makes a good beginning and a good end for a story. Then read the directions with students.

After students have completed their papers, call on volunteers to read their stories with the beginnings and ends they wrote.

Informal Assessment

Ask students to make up a good beginning sentence for this topic: *Bad weather while on vacation.*

Assess and Reteach

Is the student able to: identify the beginning, middle, and end of a story?	Reteach by allowing pre- and early production students to pantomime or draw their responses.
write beginning and end sentences?	Reteach using the Reteach Activity on TE page 437.

Name_____ Date_____

Beginning or End?

Read each sentence. If it belongs at the beginning of a story, write its number in the Beginning box. If it belongs at the end of a story, writes its number in the End box.

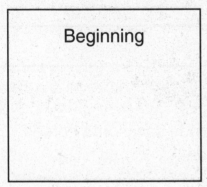

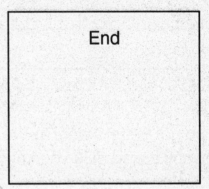

1. Did I ever tell you about Great Uncle Pete?

2. That was the last time anybody ever saw Old Bear Claw.

3. I'll never do that again!

4. There once was a very strange family.

5. Living at the top of a mountain has its problems, let me tell you!

6. That's how leopards got their spots.

7. Once I visited an old mine in a Western town.

8. In every life, there is one special moment.

9. Finally, things were back to normal.

10. Let me tell you about something that happened last year.

Name_____ Date_____

Finish the Story

Read the part of the story below. Make up a good beginning sentence for it. Make up a good ending sentence for it. Write them on the lines.

Beginning sentence: _____

_____

_____

When we got there, I went to the barn. Lin and I saw some horses. The cowboy asked, "Do you know how to ride?"

"No," I said.

Lin said, "A little."

"No problem," said the cowboy. "By the end of the day, you will be able to ride."

"Wow!" I said.

Then he helped us onto our horses and led us around the corral.

End sentence: _____

_____

_____

Introduce this lesson before Pupil Edition pages 446–461.

I. PREWRITE
Oral Warm Up

Objectives:
- Generate ideas for a story
- Ask and respond to thoughtful questions

TPR

Whole Group Oral Language Activity

Choose a book students have recently read and display the illustrations as you name the main character, the character's personality, and things the character can do. Then give a two- or three sentence summary of the plot. Ask: *Is it true or make-believe? Where does the character live?* Choose another book and ask a volunteer to describe the characters. They can also tell what happened in words or actions.

Have volunteers make up a character and describe it, or a character they know; for example, a sibling. Then ask: *What can your character do? How does your character feel? What does your character look like?* Create a four-column chart labeled: *Character, Looks Like, Personality, Can Do.* Note students' responses on the chart. Then invite a volunteer to say a sentence using the information for a character on the chart.

Graphic Organizer

Blackline Master 111

Objectives:
- Use a graphic organizer to describe a character
- Choose a character for a story

Materials: Blackline Master 111; pencils

Pre-Production and Early Production

Speech Emergence

Intermediate and Advanced Fluency

Introduce the Writing Mode

Explain that students will write a story about a character that is either make-believe or real. Point out that thinking about a main character is a good starting point for making up a story. Model describing a character for a made-up story. (*Example: My character is Mona. She is 8 years old . She is thin and has big brown eyes. Mona feels shy around new people, but she is funny and likes to sing.*)

Scaffolded Writing Instruction

Using Blackline Master 111, have students draw pictures in the boxes. Then they can use the pictures to act out ideas about their characters.

Have students label their pictures with words or phrases. Encourage them to show several things their character can do.

Ask students to draw and name their character. Then ask them to write sentences in the boxes to describe their character.

Research and Inquiry: Use a Thesaurus

Remind students that they can use a thesaurus to find different ways of saying the same thing. Write the word *funny* on the board. Invite a volunteer to use alphabetical order to find the word *funny* in a thesaurus. Then, if a computer is available, model how to use the thesaurus feature on a computer.

II. DRAFT

Objectives:
- Use sequence strategies to organize ideas
- Begin drafting a story

Focus on Writing a Story

Point out that students will tell about something that happens to their characters in their stories. Review that their stories can be make-believe or based on something real, and that they can be funny, exciting, scary, or silly. Explain that all stories have a beginning, a middle, and an ending. Write the following idea for a story and read it aloud:

Mona was shy when she moved to her new school.
Mona's father convinced her to sing at the school talent show.
Mona wasn't shy about singing.
Mona's song was wonderful. She made new friends.

Have volunteers identify the beginning, middle, and end of the story and write the words in front of the story parts. Then ask students: *During which part of the story did I introduce my character?* (the beginning) Ask: *What is Mona's problem? What is she like?* (She is shy.) Ask students: *What can Mona do?* (sing) Invite volunteers to invent the ending. Then ask volunteers to act out each part of the story.

TPR

Blackline Master 112
Materials: pencils, crayons

Scaffolded Writing Instruction

Pre-Production and Early Production

Use Blackline Master 112 to help students draft a beginning, middle, and end to their story.

Blackline Master 113
Speech Emergence

Using Blackline Master 113, guide students to draw pictures and write words and phrases to write a title that names their character, and to show what happens in the beginning, middle, and end of their story.

Intermediate and Advanced Fluency

Students may begin to write a story. Stories have characters who make things happen or solve a problem. Remind students to use descriptions to tell about their characters and the setting.

III. REVISE

Objectives:
- Revise a story
- Add ideas and descriptive words to a story

Focus on Elaboration

Write the following sentences on the board and read them aloud.

Jamal was tired.
He needed a place to sleep.
He walked into the building.
Jamal fell asleep.

TPR

Have students identify the beginning, middle, and end of the story.

Tell students that the building was a barn and ask them to suggest how they could describe it (an old red barn). Ask: *What words could we add that would tell how tired Jamal was?* (awfully, very) Prompt students to give more details by asking: *Is there another word for walked?*

Scaffolded Instruction for Revising

Pre-Production and Early Production
Blackline Master 112

Have students revise their work by drawing, adding details, and by using color. Ask them to see if their characters look the same in each picture, or if their characters show different feelings in some of the pictures.

Speech Emergence
Blackline Master 113

Use students' work on Blackline Master 113 to help them elaborate on their stories. Ask them to add words and phrases that will help readers visualize their stories.

Intermediate and Advanced Fluency

Students may revise their stories by adding details to describe or clarify.

Technology Link

Have students work with a partner to type their stories on a computer. Discuss that they can use the FIND and REPLACE feature to replace a describing word like *big* that they have used more than twice.

IV. REVISE • PEER CONFERENCING

Focus on Peer Conferencing

Objectives:
- Participate in peer conferences
- Give and receive suggestions for improvement
- Revise a story

Pair pre-production and early production students with more advanced students. Have the pre-production students use their pictures to retell their stories, and encourage them to ask for help in writing words or titles. Ask more fluent students to read their stories as they point to each word. Have early production students ask, for example: *What can your character do?* Partners of intermediate fluency can check that stories have a clear beginning, middle, and end.

Using page 255 as a guide, write and read a checklist for each language proficiency level on the chalkboard, so students can refer to them as they hold their peer conferences.

V. PROOFREAD

Focus on English Conventions

Objectives:
- Demonstrate comprehension of proofreading strategies
- Use Adjectives That Tell What Kind or How Many

Blackline Master 114

Objective: Use adjectives that tell what kind or how many.

[**Answers:** A. 1. scary, 2. huge, 3. icy, 4. bad; B. 1. Three, 2. Several, 3. few, 4. many; C. 1. delicious, 2. many, 3. cheerful, 4. some]

Say and write the following sentences:

The town has a beautiful river.
Many boats were in the river.

Point to the first sentence and ask: *What kind of river is it?* (beautiful) Explain that *beautiful* is an adjective that describes the noun *river*. Read the second sentence. Ask: *How many boats were in the river?* (many) Explain that *many* is an adjective that tells about number. Ask volunteers to suggest different adjectives that tell what kind and how many.

Have students complete Blackline Master 114 to practice the grammar skill. Ask students to proofread their work. Remind students that checking for spelling errors is an important part of proofreading.

Begin a Describing Words spelling list on the chalkboard. As students
ask for help spelling describing words, first help them sound out the
word, and then list it on the board. Students may refer to the list to check
their spelling, and also to give them ideas for their stories.

VI. PUBLISH

Objectives: Prepare a final
copy of a story and give a
dramatic reading of a story.

Use page 458 as a guide and write and read aloud a checklist for each
language proficiency level. Encourage students to use the checklist as
they prepare their speeches.

Story Theater

TPR

Place students in small mixed language-level groups to practice
reading and dramatizing their stories. Suggest that students who drew
illustrations display their drawings before each part of the story they
act out. Encourage students to ask others to act out parts in their
dramatizations. Ask students to speak clearly, use gestures and
expressions, and to use sounds to help them make an interesting
presentation. They may also choose to assemble a few simple props.

After the groups have practiced, hold a class Story Theater. Remind
listeners to listen quietly and to clap when a presentation is finished.
You may wish to invite another class to become part of the audience.

Extension

Tape record students' practices or final performances for later review.
Keep the tapes in a class audio library.

TPR

Adapt the suggestions on pages 216–217 to generate activities that
will bring out the talents of students at all proficiency levels.

VII. LISTENING, SPEAKING, VIEWING, REPRESENTING

Informal Assessment

When assessing students' learning, you will need to adapt your
expectations of what constitutes an appropriate response. For example,
you may wish to have students act out or draw a response to a verbal
or written prompt rather than having them give a traditional answer.
Assess by the clarity of the beginning, middle, and end.

Name_____ Date_____

Character Ideas

Draw the main character of your story. Show what the person looks like. Show something about his or her personality. Show something he or she can do. Then write words, phrases, or sentences to add detail.

My Character

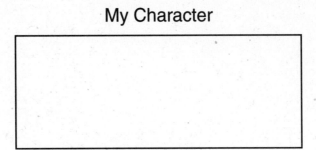

Looks Like: Personality: Can Do:

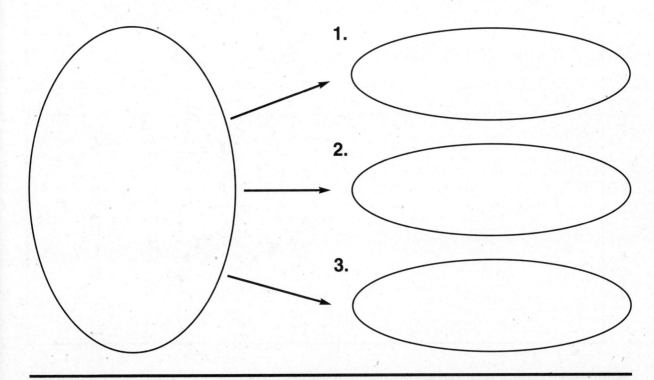

1.

2.

3.

Name_____ Date_____

Story Pictures

Think about what your character does. Draw pictures to show a beginning, a middle, and an end. Show details and color in your drawings.

1.

Beginning

2.

Middle

3.

End

Name_____ Date_____

Story Parts

Think about what happens to your character. Tell what happens in the beginning, middle, and end. Use words, phrases, and sentences to tell the story. Draw pictures and use colors to help tell your story.

Story Title: _____

The Beginning

The Middle

The End

Name_____ Date _____

Adjectives that Tell *What Kind* and *How Many*

A. Draw a line under the adjective that tells *what kind*. Then write the word.

1. Mr. Grieg was a scary man. _____

2. He drove a huge truck. _____

3. I stared into his icy eyes. _____

4. Then I realized I was having a bad dream. _____

B. Draw a line under the adjective that tells *how many*. Then write the word.

1. Three of us went to the store. _____

2. Several people were shopping. _____

3. I dropped a few boxes. _____

4. I have done this many times. _____

C. Write an adjective from the box that fits in each sentence.

delicious	many	some	cheerful

1. The food at the diner was _____.

2. I have eaten there _____ times.

3. I always feel _____ after eating.

4. _____ people feel sleepy after they eat.